OH SHIT

A JOURNEY FROM CHAOS TO CONSCIOUSNESS

NICHOLE SYLVESTER

OH SHIFT

Edited by Sarah Fox and Emily Hogenson

Cover and book design by Regina Wamba

Back cover photography by Debora Giannone

ISBN-13: 978-1544822921

I DEDICATE THIS BOOK TO...

Amy Marie Trujillo

The tragic loss of your life helped me to find my own.
I am forever grateful to you even though I have never met you.
I honor you with this book, my work and my continued
devotion to helping women heal.

Chanel Gia Sylvester

You were the first person to teach me love without wounding. You saved
me in so many ways. Your pure love called me to grow and heal so I
could become a better mother in order to show you a way of life
I only dreamed of. I love you more than you'll ever know.
Unconditionally. Thank you love bug.

DEEP GRATITUDE

To my parents Tina and David who I now know did their absolute best with what they knew. I love you both and I'm grateful for the life I've led and the lessons I've learned. Thank you.

To my editor Sarah Fox who kept it real with me and helped me dig deeper to truly honor my story. I couldn't have done this without you, truly. Thanks to Emily for her contribution to edits. Regina Wamba you are magic, thank you for bringing my book cover to life in such a powerful way.

Thank you to women who have held me physically and energetically over the years (and now) as I transform. Andrea, who has reminded me of my strength when I didn't feel I could go on anymore. Mandy, we've been through it all and now we're biz besties doing big things! Grateful. Renee (Fluff) you're always there for me and you're adventurous spirit reminds me to go lightly. Anabel, you've taught me so much about healing, receiving, sisterhood and BEing the Queen of my life. Kirsty Spraggon for leading the way as a truth teller. To women who have supported and love me: Erika, Amber, Lecia, Kylie and Anita. Thank you Elena and Amanda for reading this memoir before anyone else.

Grateful for the men in my life who've supported me on this

journey: Daniel for unconditional support and teaching me many lessons, including receptivity and trust. Mike, for always believing in me and being an amazing friend from day one. Eszylfie, for being a mentor, friend and teaching me so much about leadership and honoring potential. Sean, for showing up when I needed help most. Dominik, for helping me grow.

Special thanks to Dr. Michael Bernard Beckwith for your wisdom, teachings and support on my path to awakening. Lori Harder for your strength and brilliance as a leader, I honor you.

Tons of appreciation to my Executive Assistant, Quin - THANK YOU x100.

Lots of love to my clients (past, present and future) for trusting me and choosing me to be a guide on your sacred path. You make my life so beautiful and fulfilling. Thank you.

DISCLAIMER

The memoir you are about read is my story, all events are true but all names have been changed.

I am in no way, shape or form giving medical advice. The results shared in my story are highly personal, like most things in life. I am not suggesting you do what I have done. I am simply sharing my story to promote hope and happiness in the lives of others.

Some of the stories in this book are graphic and possibly triggering.

Read at your own risk. xo

OH
SHIT

PROLOGUE

As I listened intently to the woman on the other end of the phone, I could hear *him* complaining about me in the background. I did my best to tune it out because there was nothing I could do about it. "I'm sorry, ma'am. Could you try back another time? Right now I'm busy."

As soon as I hung up, Dean yelled out, "Make me something to eat."

How can this man eat right now? My nerves were shot from all our fighting.

"Alright," I responded, mindful of my tone as, just last week, I landed in the emergency room for speaking back to him. I hated when he barked orders at me; I wanted to tell him to get off his ass and make it himself, but I might not walk away from the kitchen after that.

Opening the fridge, I decided on pizza and pulled it out to reheat it.

Since returning home from the hospital with ten staples at the crown of my scalp, he hadn't allowed me to leave with our daughter. He knew I wanted to escape, but he wasn't allowing it. Eventually he'd loosen up and leave me along with Gia. I just hoped I could survive that long without pissing him off.

Waiting on his pizza to heat up, I realized my hands were shaky, so I decided to take a Xanax. As I went to my bag to pull out the medicine bottle, it hit me:

I could leave right now.

My heart palpitated as I processed what I was considering. I could put him to sleep with Xanax and leave with Gia.

Oh shit! I can really do this, I thought. *But can I pull this off?*

With the prescription bottle in my hand, I felt frantic. I walked back to the pizza, removed the two slices of pepperoni pizza from the toaster oven, and placed them on the cool plate. I stared at the pizza on the counter top. My mind was moving so quickly. *Can I do this?*

I was bombarded with imagery of Dean catching me as I attempted to leave and beating me to death. So much was at risk, and I was scared. I knew that things were spiraling out of control between us. I had to try. This was my chance.

While I plotted my getaway, Dean was growing impatient. "Where's my food?"

"It's coming. Sorry. I was deciding what to make."

It was time to get to work if I was going to do this. I had to give him enough to get him to fall into a deep sleep, and since he was triple my size, I figured I'd give him triple the dose I'd take. Suddenly I worried if the hot food would interfere with the drug efficacy. It was worth a try.

"Make me hot tea, too."

Perfect, I thought. *I'll add it to that, too.* I broke up one pill into his tea and added honey. I used a spoon to taste it. It was sweet enough that I couldn't taste a thing. I crushed another two pills on the granite countertop using the bottom of the tea mug. I looked into the living room to see if he was still sitting down, and he was. Next, I scattered the blue powder beneath the cheese on his slices of pizza. Luckily, though the pill was small, it packed a punch. This would do as long as he consumed all of it.

I gathered all my strength to keep my hands steady as I handed him the plate. "Here you go. Let me know if you want more."

As he sat up to eat his food, he had no clue what I was planning, and suddenly I saw his innocence. Rather than feeling happy, I was hit with overwhelming sadness for what I had done. But it was too late. As I watched him take his first bite I wondered if I had I become just like him?

I loved him. I never wanted any of this. If he weren't keeping us prisoners in the home, I wouldn't have to take such drastic measures to leave.

As I watched him eat the pizza and take a long sip of the chamomile tea, I realized I accepted that I may never see him again. As he dozed off on the sofa, I questioned whether I had the courage to grab my daughter and run out. If he caught me, I was surely dead, but if I stayed, I knew I didn't have long.

As I watched him doze off on the sofa, I made my choice.

CHAPTER 1

My vision was blurred from the tears as I tugged at my mom. "Please, Mommy! Please don't leave! He's going to do it again! Pleeease…" She continued to the door, dismissing my pleading. She had just started working the overnight shift at the factory in Downingtown.

Dressed in her white uniform and hair net, she'd leave just before we went to sleep, giving us a kiss goodnight. She'd kiss my little brother, sister, and me on the cheek with an, "I love you." I knew she loved us; that's why I was hurt and confused when I told her what was happening and she left us anyway.

I'd pull on her jacket and follow her to the door with my cries. She ignored my request. I knew she had to work, she was paying the bills for all of us, of course, but I didn't care at this point. I knew she loved us, so why didn't she listen?

"Oh stop it, Nikki. I talked to him about it. You'll be fine." Those words felt like betrayal as a seven-year-old little girl. I watched her walk off the front porch and out to the car. *I can't believe she is leaving me—leaving us! How could she do this to me?* I sobbed harder. *I'm scared, and she doesn't care.* I knew she had to go. However, I couldn't grasp her reasoning. Eventually, drained and defeated, I went to crawl into bed with my little sister.

Hours later, I was awoken by my dad. He urgently loaded the three of us in the car on the bitter cold November night. I could hear the music coming from the front speakers, but the old car was much louder. The thin cloth from the interior roof was falling down so that it hung just over my Dad's head. I hated the car; it embarrassed me at school because the other kids would make fun of it as my parents pulled up to pick us up.

As we continued down the expressway, I saw the familiar orange, neon light of the Valley Forge Hotel, and I knew right away we were driving to the city. Suddenly, I felt nauseous, and my legs were shaking. My dad was taking us to get his fix, and there was nothing I could do about it.

We lived forty minutes from Philadelphia in the western suburbs of Chester County, Pennsylvania. My siblings were sleeping; I felt I had to keep them safe when we went to these places, but I also wanted to keep my dad safe. I was scared he would die, and something would happen to us.

Soon we pulled off 76 Expressway and into North Philly. I recognized this area from our other trips. The poverty-stricken neighborhood was made up of narrow streets lined with small, rundown row homes. Cars were parked along the streets, nearly touching one another; some of them were even parked on the sidewalk. I once saw my father get robbed here; I'd seen fights and watched the ways of the street from the back seat of our car with a pit in my stomach. In the warmer months, these streets were filled with people, yet tonight it was different. The streets were empty with no movement in the darkness; it felt eerie.

We came to a stop sign, and my dad rolled down his window and waved. Looking over, I saw a tall man in an oversized, black, hooded jacket walk off one of the nearby porches. It was so dark, and his hood was so big that I could barely make out his face, reminding me of the grim reaper. The man stopped to check the surroundings before proceeding and then walked to a broken part of the sidewalk where he reached down to grab a small bag from beneath the broken cement slab. Then he approached our car.

The exchange took no more than a minute. *Thank God. We are safe.*

My dad drove for a few minutes until he found a parking spot. By this time, my brother was awake. We both knew to stay quiet; mostly I think we were bracing ourselves.

In the front seat, my dad was doing his thing. He had a syringe, a metal spoon just like the kind of spoon we used for cereal, and a bottle of liquid he used to clean his needle. I understood why he did this; there was so much on the news about HIV. Even my dad knew people who had caught HIV from sharing needles. He emptied the contents of the tiny white bag and held the lighter under the spoon to melt the mixture.

From my angle, I couldn't see him inject himself, but I knew where the marks were on his arm. My mom would argue with my father when she noticed these marks. I could tell he was feeling the effects because he would typically fall to the side or get really quiet. This time he fell over against the driver side door, directly in front of me. By this point, my entire body was shaking, my stomach was in knots, and I felt like I was going to throw up in my seat. My brother's big hazel eyes were wide as he peered into the front of the car at my dad.

It was really quiet for what seemed like forever with no movement from my dad. Beginning to worry, I called out to him, "Dad?"

Nothing.

Not much was happening besides a few other cars passing us. We waited.

"Daddy..." My brother spoke hesitantly. This woke my little sister who was sitting in her car seat between us. A few moments later, car lights pulled up behind us and parked.

Oh no, I thought.

I heard two car doors shut, and a man walked up to the driver's side window with a flashlight. I was relieved to see the hat and badge; I knew it was a cop. The other cop was standing next to my brother's window.

The officer knocked on my dad's window. "Wake up. Roll down your window."

Nothing. Now I was crying. My brother and I were yelling, "Daddy, wake up!" My sister was crying, too. I began to panic; my dad was dead. He wasn't waking up.

The police guided us to unlock the door and get out of the car. We unbuckled our seatbelts and listened. The officers asked us to get into their squad car. I didn't want to leave my dad. I resisted; I couldn't leave him.

"Is he breathing? Please help him, hurry! He needs help!" I screamed through my terror as the reality of losing my dad sunk in.

"He'll be fine. We're gonna get him to the hospital." This soothed our cries as we piled into the back seat.

Another cop car pulled up with an ambulance following behind it. The loud sirens and bright red lights brought with them a feeling of safety in this moment. A feeling of relief swept over me, and I knew my dad was going to make it.

Soon we arrived at the police station where they called my grandmom, and we waited for her to give us a ride home. This wasn't the first time I had to call someone to pick us up, but I always called my mother's mom, Dolly. She always came through for us, even though it was the middle of the night, and most times, she had work in the morning herself. She was my safe person. As we sat quietly on the metal chairs beneath the harsh florescent light, I thought about my mom and sadness came over me. I was hurting. I didn't want to live like this anymore. I told myself it was over; this time my mom would listen, and this wouldn't happen again. She couldn't ignore this.

Sadly, I was wrong. I learned that addiction eats away love and logic. My parents would argue when the grocery money was spent on drugs. The fights were loud and sometimes violent. The three of us children would run into the kitchen for the landline to call 9-1-1 as we yelled for our dad to stop hurting Mommy. From time to time, my mom was left with a puffy lip or black eye. This made me feel like I should hate my dad for hurting her, but I couldn't. I hated how they behaved. I hoped that one day they would love us enough to stop all of it.

In time, my mom began to develop an addiction of her own to deal with my dad's struggle. My mother chose alcohol, and her choice seemed more social and harmless—at first. However, I sensed I was also losing my mom.

One night we stayed up late waiting for my mom to come home. I could tell it was later than usual because infomercials were now playing on the TV. The familiar fear began to sink in. Where was she? No one else appeared to be worried, but I sensed something was going on. Then the phone rang. Our babysitter, Marissa, woke up from where she had drifted off on the recliner, and she hurried across the dining room to the kitchen and picked up the phone. I could hear her; she was concerned.

"Okay, I'm only the sitter. I don't have a car, and I'm here with her kids."

Who was she talking to? She got off the phone and returned to the living room.

"Nikki, I need you to call your grandmother for me."

I could tell something was wrong, but she couldn't tell me what had happened. I picked up the phone and dialed my grandmom,

Dolly. Marissa held her hand out, gesturing for me to pass over the phone.

My grandmom arrived and stayed overnight with us. My mother was arrested for a DUI. She wrecked our minivan. She crashed into a telephone pole on the way home from the bar. She fell unconscious, and when another driver found her, he called for help.

Thankfully, she was okay, although she had to sleep in the holding cell at the police station overnight. When we drove to pick her up the next morning, she only had a few bruises and busted lip. This was the end of me feeling safe about my mother leaving home. I then began to worry about losing both parents. I lived in fear. I felt abandoned by their choices to escape through their vices. Didn't they realize we *needed* them?

Over the years, I asked my mom if she would consider stopping her drinking. She'd brush me off, denying her behavior and ignoring my concerns. "Oh, I'm fine, Nikki. Stop it."

Although my mom seemed happier when she was enjoying a beer, it didn't feel good to me. I felt like she couldn't see me or hear me. When I was right in front of her, I could see that she couldn't understand me. She was drunk, and even at a young age, I had this feeling that my words weren't reaching her. I began to hate her drinking. There was a sense of betrayal when she was drunk because I felt both of my parents were gone.

The dynamic between my parents and the choices they made to quiet their own demons led our extended family to disconnect from us. The invitations to birthday parties and holiday gatherings slowed to an eventual stop, and soon the same happened with friends at schools.

In the small towns we lived in, as we bounced from one school district to another, there was gossip about my family. The neighbors saw the police visiting our home because of frequent fights between my parents. My siblings and I missed school often. My little brother, who was just a year younger than I, once stood up in class and said that my Dad was using drugs at home. Our chaotic lifestyle was no secret.

Other parents didn't want their children around kids like us. It stung, but I was embarrassed by my life, and I didn't blame their parents. Mondays at school were the worst, as I listened to my friends laugh and recall their sleepovers that I wasn't invited to. Some of the children told me the truth. The awkward conversation went something like, "My mom said I can't hang out with you, but I still want to be your friend. Okay?" I pretended I didn't care. I repeated my mantra: I don't care. I don't care. I don't care.

My parents' addictions were isolating us even more. I hoped that it would get better, but time would prove me wrong.

CHAPTER 2

"Lights out in ten minutes." The guard's voice blared over the hall speakers as I thumbed through my notebook. My probation officer suggested I write down my feelings to process them. His suggestion was given before I arrived in juvenile hall, but I wasn't patient enough to try this practice at home, even though I needed it. Our home was like a pinball machine, and we rolled through our small home, pressing buttons and lighting up one another until someone lost it. I typically ran off with friends to get high or drunk instead of going home to get involved.

I closed the composition book and tucked it beneath my flat, stiff pillow before situating myself beneath the itchy wool blanket. My eyes closed but my mind continued replaying the weeks before I wound up here. There were many chances to behave differently, but I didn't. As I lay in my cell taking note of the pivotal moments where I went further down the wrong path, I had perfect vision; I saw my mistakes.

Over three weeks had passed since I was arrested for cutting off my house arrest ankle bracelet and leaving my parents' home in the middle of the night. Each night as I lay in the dark, my mind drifted to the events of previous weeks. I knew I wasn't living my best life, but I didn't intend on landing in lockup. I wanted to do better, but I didn't know how to stop running away—both physically and emotionally.

Before I got locked up, I spent a lot of my time on country roads in the middle of nowhere where cars didn't pass for hours. I'd head out with my girlfriends to meet up with a group of high schoolers, enjoying the feeling of my skin exposed to the spring air after having been covered in layers all winter. It was a low-key night, and we were getting as drunk as possible to make our mundane lives more entertaining. The seven of us passed the 100-proof bottle of Southern Comfort around the circle, almost ceremonially. We drank until that country road became a fun place, yet when we started getting bitten by mosquitoes, it was time to head back.

Our plan was to go back to Rachel's place and smoke and sleep. My friend Rachel was driving her Ford Explorer, and suddenly she jerked the wheel left and right in an attempt to make us laugh. I could feel the back tires sliding on the loose rocks beneath us until suddenly the SUV jerked left and the vehicle rolled, tossing the four of us around like laundry in a dryer. I braced myself, waiting for the vehicle to land.

"Oh shit! You guys okay?" someone yelled out from the car following us home.

Everyone was alive, thank God, but the Explorer landed on the driver's side, and I was sitting behind the driver. The sheer shock of the accident sobered me up some. My prickly panic dissolved into a wave of relief when I knew everyone was okay. However, my drunkenness returned as I crawled out of the passenger's side door that was now facing the stars. As we stood outside waiting for the tow truck, we considered what we would tell the police.

"Nikki, your arm is bleeding!" Rachel's tone startled me, and I almost felt afraid to look down, yet I glanced to see blood on my forearm, hand, and clothing. There were small shards of glass sticking out from my arm. I thought, *So much blood. Do not panic. Do not panic.*

I knew the alcohol had thinned my blood, which made the bleeding worse. The window next to me shattered during the accident, and my arm hit the glass. I hadn't felt the pain right away due to shock. The ambulance and police arrived ten minutes later, and I was taken to the hospital for stitches. It was there that I was informed of my underage drinking charges. My upcoming court case for truancy came to mind, and I knew this wouldn't help my cause one bit. The months leading up to the accident felt almost unbearable. All I wanted to do was get high and check out of my reality, which was against the law. The school reported me, and I was summoned to court.

After the accident, I didn't change my ways as my court date approached. I was back out drinking and getting high before the stitches were out. Deep down, I yearned for a happy and idyllic life at home where I could have dinner with my family followed by television time spent laughing and sitting together in the living room. The idea of home that I craved wasn't anything like the home I actually had. I wanted connection and someone to hear me, and I didn't have that in *my* home. My home environment stung me, and it made me want to run away as soon as I arrived back there. At least when I couldn't take it anymore or when I had nowhere else to go, I knew I could walk to my grandmother's place just two miles away. Oftentimes, that's exactly what I did.

One evening after an intense clash with my dad, I left home and began walking to my grandmother's place fighting back tears the entire way. I didn't want to cry; I didn't want my Dad to win. This was back when I believed stuffing my emotions inside was the same as not having any. It was eight p.m. when I finally arrived, and my older cousin James was just leaving for a party. James lived with my Grandmother. James had been in and out of lockup since he was thirteen years old, and while he was considered trouble, I liked to hang with him.

"Come with me," he yelled out from the car, signaling me to get in. so

I hopped into the passenger seat and we were off. I still had a lump in my throat from the fight I walked out on back at my house. *A drink could make this go down a bit easier*, I thought.

The party was a ten-minute drive away at the edge of town in a small Cape Cod style home. It was filled with people smoking and talking, and there was a keg of beer out back in the small, dark yard that was lined with tall trees. Later that night, James said he had to run somewhere and asked me to stay at the party. I knew that meant he was going to buy some sort of drug that I wouldn't do. Smoking crack was something he'd begun doing and was ashamed of, and he didn't admit it openly, but word was that he was hooked. This rumor was from the people who sold it around town.

I agreed to stay to avoid confrontation, and I went to sit on the sofa with a fresh cup of Coors Light. I felt slightly out of place without James there, but I didn't want to go home after what happened. I decided to drink faster.

Robert, one of James's friends, came to sit with me, and he had a big, bright smile on his face. He said, "You look lost sitting over here alone." I laughed, but I knew he was right since I did feel lost. Robert and I hung out for the next three hours, waiting for James to return. We laughed a lot, and I decided I liked the way I felt important around him.

After the party, Robert and I began hanging out more often. Eventually, we started hooking up, and people around town started to wonder what was going on, yet due to a six-year age difference, we decided to keep our relationship private. It was illegal since he was twenty-two. Besides, we didn't know what we were doing just yet ourselves; we only knew that we liked being together, and we agreed that no one else had to know.

Reflecting on Robert made me uncomfortable. I shifted on the hard bedding, attempting to find comfort, I wondered if I'd be able to sleep at all. I was nervous for my court date the next morning, and after considering what I'd done, I wasn't sure I deserved a second chance. I knew I didn't want to stay in here.

Yet, when I closed my eyes as recent events swirled almost obsessively in my mind, I remembered the day I was originally placed on house arrest. I knew it would be difficult with my family dynamic. Regret moved through me as I remembered my grandmother's advice, "Nikki, it's only thirty days. Get past this, and you get a fresh start. Let everything your parents say roll off your back."

I nodded as tears rolled down my cheeks, feeling completely trapped by this arrangement. I knew the two of them would provoke me even more now that I had no choice but take it. Their words pushed my anxiety over the edge. Yet, I gathered up my strength and thought about the freedoms I would have thirty-one days from now.

The first week on house arrest was somewhat tolerable. I was able to stay in my room and isolate myself. I began to think it wouldn't be so bad after all. Robert and I were still talking on the phone, and we both missed one another. I asked him to come over late at night and meet me in the backyard, and he did. The first two nights when he came over, we'd talk for an hour in the driveway, and then he'd walk home. I was dying for more of a connection. I wanted more time and more touch. It had been two days since Robert visited when my dad finally came barreling down basement stairs.

"Don't fuck with me, Nikki! Bring your friends here again and see what happens," he said. As he continued to rant, I could see the veins swelling in his neck. When he reached this point of rage, he'd spit with every word he spoke. I got scared when this happened. I didn't say a word. It had been a while since my dad hit me; I didn't want to start it again. When he went back, I could hear the muffled bangs of cabinets slamming shut and then my mother's voice chiming in.

This is when I would usually leave, yet this time I couldn't. I was trapped, and I had to deal with whatever came my way until he decided to stop. I paced my room and felt the anxious thoughts getting louder as irrationality won me over. I didn't want to be there; I didn't care what happened next, not in that moment. That night, when the pressure became too much, I cut the tracking monitor off of my leg and left. As soon as the monitor fell to the ground, I realized I made a mistake, but it was too late. I had friends pick me up, and I ran off with them for a few days to Ocean City, Maryland.

Within a week, I was back in Parkesburg with Robert. I was now technically considered a runaway. There was a warrant out for my arrest. Between the two of us, we had enough money to stay at a dingy motel twenty minutes from my parents' place, and as Robert checked us in, it hit me that our relationship was illegal. I also realized that I was homeless, and we only had enough cash for two nights at the motel. Walking across the gravel lot to our room, I felt dirty. I knew I had to call my parents soon. I wondered if there was any chance I could make this better.

Our hotel room reeked of mildew and cigarette smoke, which didn't surprise me. Mostly people who were up to no good used this motel: hookers, cheaters, drug dealers, underage drinkers, and runaways. I had been there for two of those categories. A group of my friends and I had all chipped in a few times to have a motel party here so we could smoke, drink, and have fun during the winter months. However, this time, it felt even more dismal. The only positive in the situation was the alone time I got to spend with Robert. It was nice to have someone around me who loved me. Finally, I felt I found someone to care for me and support me, and I was infatuated. We ordered a cheesesteak from the attached bar. We each ate half while sitting on the lumpy bed. We cuddled up while watching the grainy, black-and-white television screen.

A loud bang on our door caused us to jump out of bed. Within an instant, the hotel room doors flew open, and officers flooded in with their weapons aimed directly at us. There must have been six men with their rifles pointed at us while they screamed for us to put our hands up. I quickly realized that they must have thought Robert kidnapped me, or, at the very least, heavily influenced me to come with him. They seemed to be directing their anger towards him, which was strange as I was the troublemaker in the situation.

The handcuffs were digging into my wrists as I sat in the back of the police car, and I knew I screwed myself over.

The alone time in lockup led me to talk with God. I began to pray for the first time. I was confused by who God was as I didn't believe in the God I had learned about in my great-grandmother's Catholic church. That God didn't approve of gays or women who had abortions, so I didn't trust that God. He seemed angry. Plus, I knew He wouldn't like me at this rate. However, I was desperately wondering whether a greater God might exist who would forgive me and give me more chances. There was a Bible in the main room, and I began to skim through it during community room time. Back in the quiet of my room, I made deals with God. I thought, *If you get me out of this, I promise to never run away again.*

I considered the plans I had for my new life if God helped me out. I imagined working in a powerful position, going to college, and someday becoming an all-around badass woman. I wanted to change the world, although I didn't know how, and I felt I was born for something great. I continued my conversations with God, although the connection to my God still didn't feel quite real. I still couldn't get over the judgmental signs posted in front of my Catholic church regarding women and gays. I just didn't believe in a God who didn't love everyone or wanted people to treat another human poorly. Yet, I was still willing to test out my bargaining skills with him, and I thought I would give him a chance if he were willing to give me one in exchange.

The next morning, I awoke to the guard at my door; it was time to make my way back to the courthouse for my hearing. My chest tightened as I remembered my fate now rested in the hands of a woman I barely knew. I had heard many stories while in juvie, and some of those stories involved my appointed judge locking up girls for nearly one year for only minor offenses. I damaged county property and had proved myself irresponsible at home. I wasn't expecting her to let me off the hook for this. My deals with God were still up in the air. Would he come through and salvage our relationship?

With cuffs and shackles around my wrists and ankles, I struggled to get into the back of the sheriff's van. I rode along through Delaware County and into West Chester, where we parked in the back alley of the juvenile court. I went into the disappointingly familiar waiting cell. As I sat on the flat metal bench that lined the cell, I prepared myself for the worst-case scenario. I hoped for the best, but I didn't want to feel the excruciating crush of holding out hope only to unexpectedly go away for nine months.

I was served a brown paper bag lunch consisting of a cheese sandwich and four saltine crackers. I wasn't sure, but it felt like seven hours had passed in the cell. Finally, the steel door opened, and the constable signaled me to get up. I glanced at the clock on the wall; I was in the waiting cell from nine a.m. to three thirty p.m. There was another girl who had left for court before me, and when she left and never returned, it briefly sparked my optimism. I imagined how it might feel to get sentenced to six more months away from home, but quickly I pushed that thought away and focused on getting out. It was go time. *God, do you hear me?*

Reaching the courtroom, I broke down when I saw my grandmother. I felt so close to freedom, yet it wasn't guaranteed. I wanted to go home with her so badly my stomach ached. I had planned to remain more composed and tough and to take responsibility for my actions. Yet, I couldn't hold back the emotion. I hated hurting my grandmother; she had enough of it already. The judge asked me to share what I learned during my time in the center and how I felt. I wiped my cheeks, moist with my tears, and I told her I would appreciate another chance to change my life and get my GED.

God must've listened because the judge granted a miracle that day. She allowed me to leave with my grandmother. Only this time, I was now sentenced to ninety days of house arrest with probation and fines to pay off the destroyed monitoring device.

I was just focused on getting to my house and seeing my friends and my boyfriend, if he and I were still a *thing*. I imagined that he had altogether moved on because nearly a month had passed since he was handcuffed due to my choices. When I finally arrived home, my mom was happy to see me, but my dad didn't speak to me. I went into my bedroom and found Robert's number. I called him and a few other friends.

That night, a few people came to quickly say hello, including Robert. It turns out he was still into me. I was happy, even though his family warned him against continuing our connection. After all, they were the ones that he called when he was arrested at gunpoint with a sixteen-year-old. I didn't blame them, but I didn't agree. *What's age got to do with love, anyway?*

Time had passed, and I managed to stay out of trouble. I only had one close call throughout the summer, and it wasn't due to my behavior. One of my girlfriends got into a fistfight in the middle of the street next to my home. She and another woman were fighting over a man, which was typical, but luckily, they broke it up and left before police were called.

My probation officer was helpful, and he helped me stay on track. He visited me weekly at my home, and he saw firsthand how my parents spoke to me. He visited me one particular day when I was fed up and feeling defeated.

He pulled me back up by telling me, "Nichole, you can't let this penetrate you. It's just your family's communication style. They go right for your jugular every time. They want to hurt you with words, but if you know that, you know what to expect. Don't let them win."

It felt so good to have someone understand me. He was right; I could see it. It was hard for my family and friends to see it because they were either too close to the situation to see it or not close enough to see it or they too had tendencies of behaving that way too. I was no angel, but I began to realize that I had learned this behavior from my parents. My probation officer helped me get through my ninety days without sinking into depression. His weekly visits were something to look forward to. I reminded myself to keep going, and with his help, I made it through my sentence. On day ninety-one, I walked out of the courthouse feeling lighter.

CHAPTER 3

I t felt strange to have my ankle back after having showered and slept with a bulky black box on my right ankle for three months. I was excited to get out into the world again to spend time with my friends and Robert. It was still warm weather, and for the first time in ages, I had time to enjoy it. The first night I was free, I went out with everyone to Creek Road, a country road where we drank and smoked and listened to blaring music. I never liked being in the middle of nowhere when I was sober. I dealt with it, but I dreamt of the days when I'd be in a high-end lounge in the city. We all stood around drinking and listening to Tupac's *All Eyez on Me* album. No one could hear our music this far out. We had twenty-two-ounce bottles of Old English malt liquor. There must've been twenty of us out there. The energy of the night felt off; I felt like I no longer belonged, but I wrote it off that I was out of sorts from being locked up for the past four months. As I downed my beer, the underlying irritation grew. I felt like I missed out on something or everyone was keeping something from me.

The night continued as the car headlights illuminated the dark woods surrounding us. Robert wasn't how I remembered him. He and I were side by side on nights out; he was my partner in crime, literally. My paranoia kicked in as I noticed him move away from me as I attempted to get closer. I doubted myself, imagining whether he was truly behaving differently. There were other girls there who it was clear he knew, even though I hadn't met them. Why didn't I know them? The cold, bitter beer wasn't enough to tame the fiery rage beginning to build. The more I drank, the more disconnected I felt. I had become visibly bothered, which was a trait of my mother's. My mom couldn't hide her feelings, not for one moment. Her emotions became visible and were quickly experienced by others.

I craved attention. I obsessed over our relationship for the past four months, and now I was being ignored by him. This emotional game hurt; I was unsure of what I was feeling, but I was certain I didn't like it, and I wanted it to stop. I didn't want to be there anymore. I imagined my first night out feeling differently, more of a celebration with a friend; he was feeling more like an enemy. As I approached him, softly touching his arm, as if to signal that I was there, he snapped his eyes at me in disgust. He shifted and moved away to continue speaking with someone else.

Confusion took over as I realized his anger. I felt lost out on the road. What happened to my friend, my lover? Fed up, I began asking friends to drive me home. As I moved through the crowd of mostly familiar faces, asking for a way home, that's when Robert paid attention.

My friend Matt was willing to take me home. As we stood there talking, I could see Robert in my peripheral vision coming toward me. *Good*, I thought.

"You're not going anywhere." His arrogance stunned me.

Disgusted by his attempt to control me, I backed away. "I'm not staying here. Not with the way you've been tonight." As I turned to walk away, I saw his eyes widen, reminding me of my father's eyes when he was consumed by his madness. Turning to find my girlfriends across the wooded lot, I heard others attempting to calm him down, but he was bigger than most, and he was known to be a fighter. No one really messed with him. Within thirty seconds, he stormed over to continue his questions. "Who do you think you're fucking with?"

At this point, I wasn't arguing back. I was afraid. I sensed he was about to lose it. Worried he'd hurt Matt out of jealousy, I backed down. His eyes revealed his rage. He became unrecognizable. Then he did something I never would have imagined he would ever do— he shoved me down on the gravel road. I could feel the cool dirt and jagged rocks scratch against my bare legs.

I could still hear him, but my hearing was warped by shock. His fit still wasn't over. My hands hurt as I pushed myself up, looking at him and expecting to find remorse. Instead, he pushed me down again, harder. Now I was crying. I didn't know what the fuck to do at that point. I just could not believe what was happening. As I looked for someone to help, I saw that others were just as shocked as I was. Soon, I saw his two friends come rushing over. As I lay on the gravel, afraid to get hurt worse, I was relieved as his boys talked him down, and though the party was not over, quietly we all drove home. Thankfully, he and I rode in separate cars. So many thoughts raced through my mind. This was so unforgivable. *No one would treat me this way. No one.* I sobbed all the way home. I was completely distraught. I wanted answers. I needed to know why. I thought this man loved me. At a minimum, he was my friend. *How could he do this to me? To us?* Curled under my covers after the drive home, still dirty from the night, I eventually cried myself asleep.

The next day, I woke up sore and stiff from the night before. I immediately thought of Robert. I wanted to hate him, but I didn't. I sobbed alone on my bed, realizing my heart and mind were conflicted. I lay back down and cried as I replayed what happened. *What did I do wrong? How did this happen to us?* I recalled the evening and found that I was jealous, but did I deserve to be shoved onto the road? I didn't know the answer.

I lifted up my covers to inspect the sore parts of my body. My knees were scratched and bloody, and the wounds had begun to scab. I cried, resisting the truth: Robert did this to my body.

With all that I felt, I hated myself for wishing that he were here with me. I wanted him to make this better. *What the hell is wrong with me?*

I felt frantic and confused as to why I was afraid of losing an abusive boyfriend. My mind said, *Fuck him*, but my heart screamed, *I need him.*

Robert obviously needed help; he didn't want to be this way. I couldn't turn my back on him so soon. Plus, I knew I could be a bitch, too. I was not totally innocent in this; I had triggered this.

That morning, I rationalized for hours until I decided to call Robert. My body felt heavy and shameful as I dialed his number. I could hear my girlfriends' voices in my head as I sat on my bedroom floor with my phone in my hand, "You deserve better, Nikki!" and "You don't need him."

The shame moved through me as I desperately wished I believed them. It wasn't enough. I needed the love. I did need him. I wasn't sure that I deserved better; I didn't think I could find better. Not now. I had to fix this first.

My heart palpitated when he answered the phone, although I was relieved that he sounded just as ashamed. I was expecting him to be happy that I called, giving him an opportunity to say sorry and make things right. He was lucky I called.

Nope. He barely said anything.

"What happened? How could you become so angry?"

He was quiet, and then he spoke in a hushed tone, "I didn't want to. You pushed me with your attitude."

I thought about it. Was I behaving like my mom when she argued with my dad until he snapped?

He continued, "I'm sorry. I didn't want to hurt you. I blacked out."

"Look, I don't like what you did; I hate it. I know we can fix this. We can both do better..."

He interrupted, "No, it's too late. Everyone saw what happened. I'm lucky I'm not in jail."

I wanted him to fight for us. "I don't care about everyone else; this isn't about them. It's about us. We can fix this." I truly believed it. I was blinded by my needy love. He must've been, too; he agreed.

My parents came to mind. I remember my dad's violence toward my mom and us, but he stopped. Robert could, too. I held onto my dad's recovery as evidence men could change, I knew the truth. Change was possible. Sure, my father still had a heated temper, but he didn't hit my mom anymore. Like my mom said, "We stick together no matter what happens." I never had someone love me like Robert. I couldn't let go yet; I loved him, so I had to try. Isn't that what love was?

I created stories in my mind to support us working out. These fantasies included the abuse never happening again and Robert proving himself to all my friends and me. I wanted this to be true. Unfortunately, it wasn't the case.

In the months to follow, there were more episodes of violence. It was as if he felt more comfortable expressing his rage. The shoving and grabbing of my arms turned into a direct punch in the face.

There were violent outbursts sparked by finding out I was spending time with guy friends, even though they were friends whom he knew. His controlling behavior was out of control; I never knew what would spark a fight as time went on. He began taking out his everyday problems on me once he was drunk.

I walked home one night alone after Robert's friend had to

pull him off me. A group of us were drinking beers and watching football. A few hours later, we were taking shots of vodka, and Robert's mood switched: he grew quiet and restless. When I tried to support him, and see if he needed to talk, he pushed me away. When he found out I was leaving, he snapped and started to accuse me of cheating on him. I denied it, which was the truth, but still, it was too late. He was too angry and that was the first night he punched me directly in my face. He hit me more than once, I was curled on the floor attempting to block his blows when his friends pulled him away from me and calmed him down. Thank God we weren't alone.

That night something shifted; I knew he wasn't going to change. He was quickly getting worse.

I knew I'd been hit in my face multiple times, but I didn't see myself yet. As his friends kept him in the kitchen, I grabbed my things and ran out of the house. Now I was walking as fast as I could uphill to my house. My right cheek felt big and sore. I could taste blood in my mouth. I could tell I'd be bruised. I couldn't wait to get home. After what happened, home felt safe.

A wave of relief came over me as I walked in the house. Robert was crazy, but so was my father. I knew he wouldn't dare come here. My mom was sitting at the table sorting through mail. She noticed me and quickly jumped up. "What happened to you!?"

I began to sob uncontrollably. "It was Robert. We got into an argument, and he went crazy." Suddenly my mom felt like my mom again, and I cried with my head on her shoulder for a few moments, and my dad came in. She explained what happened. He looked disgusted.

"Where is he?" Now my dad was pissed.

I told him I didn't know because I didn't want to make the situation worse. I'd seen my dad in enough brawls to know this wouldn't turn out well.

My dad paced around the kitchen, my mom directed, "We're calling the police. Enough is enough! I had a feeling about this…"

I didn't want to be a snitch, calling the police on someone was the ultimate weak move in the crowd I hung out with. I knew I would hear the accusations from mutual friends, but in this moment, I had enough. My body was tired, and I knew Robert needed help. My parents called the police.

The police found Robert and arrested him at his mom's place. I felt horrible. The thought of him in jail, uncomfortable and alone, pained me. I knew it was sick; I was the victim, yet I felt his suffering. My twisted feelings of love and pain consumed me.

Robert was to be released in a matter of days. The day I received a call from the police officer, who informed me he had been released, I went to the bathroom and threw up. I felt ashamed. I felt like I couldn't leave the house and see my friends for he may come around, too. Somehow I shifted from the cool chick who could hang out all night long to the sad, weak, and pathetic girl who had to hide. The heaviness of this new reality made me queasy. I couldn't drink to avoid how alone I felt—although I tried; I was unable to get anything down. I attempted to smoke a joint in the hopes I'd get my appetite back, but it was short-lived.

A few more days passed, and that's when I realized my period was nearly one week late. The realization hit me like a punch to the gut; I felt more nauseous. Doing my best to tame my frantic energy, I searched several pairs of jeans for money, throwing each pair carelessly on the floor and adding to the mess in my room. *Damn it.* I ended my search with two quarters in my hand.

My mom was sitting at the dining room table reading the newspaper with her coffee; she looked peaceful, which gave me a good feeling about asking her for a favor.

"Hey, Mom. Do you think you could give me five dollars for pizza?"

She lowered her paper. "Why don't you eat here?"

"I haven't had an appetite, and I'm craving a plain pizza slice."

Putting her paper down on the table, she responded, "Hand me my purse." She signaled to the end of the table.

She handed me the five-dollar bill, and I made my way out the door.

Instead of buying pizza, I snuck off to the pharmacy to buy a pregnancy test. I caught a glimpse of myself as I walked out of the pharmacy and thought, *Wow, you are such a fucking mess.* The angry voice in my head went on a full-blown rant. *You have remnants of a black eye as you purchase a pregnancy test, and you haven't even turned eighteen yet. Never going to get it together at this rate.*

That mean girl in my head got even louder as I sat on the toilet watching the blue lines appear on the test in front of me. I was pregnant with Robert's baby. *FUCK.*

CHAPTER 4

Planned Parenthood was a thirty-five-minute drive from where I lived. It had seemed awkward and inconvenient to get my mother to drive me into West Chester to sign for my birth control, yet that changed when I saw those blue lines on the white pregnancy test. Suddenly, my avoidance seemed so ridiculous. I hated myself for avoiding the request.

I knew if I were adamant about getting the pills, I wouldn't be dealing with a pregnancy at seventeen. Getting the pills seemed like a leisurely lunch date compared to asking my mom to help me figure out what I should do with my baby.

Robert was home, but we weren't speaking since his release. He was court ordered not to contact me. I found out from a friend that Robert was cheating on me before his arrest. While it was far from a shock, it still hurt to hear. I had a feeling, but this woman confirmed it to my friend, so now it was real. Aside from the fact that this man nearly knocked me unconscious on several occasions, his cheating and lies helped me as I worked to get over him. I didn't want to be tied to this man forever. Yes, I had trouble getting over him, but I was wise enough to know he wasn't an ideal father. Plus, I wasn't exactly mother material myself.

I felt sad for this baby; there was no way I should birth a child into the world to depend on us. Yet, there was a feeling that superseded logic. Knowing I had a baby growing in my womb gave me a feeling of not being alone. It was different than I had felt with friends or family. It was just us. This comforted me. But could I have a baby?

Reluctantly, I told my mom and grandmom about my situation and watched the disappointment move over their faces. My cousin James had already had children and was now back in jail for his involvement in a murder. The level of chaos occurring in our family was at an all-time high, and now I added to it all.

"Okay, Nikki, you've got to set up your appointment. The earlier you get it done, the better. Let's call now," my grandmom said after a long exhale.

"Get what done?" I asked

"An abortion. Get it done now, and get it out of the way to move on," my mom added in.

"I don't have the money for that, and I haven't decided."

My grandmom quickly responded, "No, I will pay for it. You've got to, Nikki. Be smarter than us."

"Other people have their babies and work it out. I can be a single mom if I wanted to."

My mom was getting frustrated. "Nikki, please. You've got your entire life ahead of you. I'm scheduling your appointment now."

They helped me set up an appointment at Planned Parenthood. There was no hesitation. It was a worthwhile investment for my grandmom since this baby would be living at her home. My grandmom was already taking care of me at this point. I went to visit my parents once or twice per week, I knew my Dad wouldn't welcome a baby.

Now that I faced the decision, I was more depressed than ever. I felt plagued by the Catholic guilt; I didn't want to burn in hell. My family didn't seem too concerned with my afterlife. I worried that my decision to not have this baby now would result in me never having a baby. Not that I planned on children, but who knew?

I feared I didn't deserve a baby again after a decision like this. My mind spun with the possibilities. I knew I could handle whatever happened. Plenty of women had babies before they were ready; it simply worked out. I knew I would be on my own. I was willing to accept that. While I played the movie in my mind of what life could be like, I imagined Robert getting help and coming back to take care of the baby and me. We would be a happy and healthy family like I always wanted. I didn't want to throw away that chance, but the chance was too slim. Robert wasn't changing anytime soon, and I had my own demons to tend to, I wasn't ready to be a mom. Finally, I gathered my courage to make the call to Planned Parenthood. As I hung up the phone, I began to cry; the grieving had begun.

It was a gloomy morning as we drove to my initial consultation. I kept reminding myself that I didn't have to decide yet. This felt like a buffer. The last time I went to the clinic was for a pap smear when I turned sixteen and started experiencing intense cramps in my lower left abdomen. I was freaked out then, but this was next level anxiety in comparison. My grandmother had already decided this was the best choice. She would shut down any discussion of an alternative ending; therefore, I couldn't share what I was experiencing.

I knew my family believed this was the right thing to do, and deep down, I did too. Robert and I were in no condition to keep the baby. I couldn't deny that a part of me saw this baby as a symbol of the love I had never experienced. I felt this baby would bring me something I needed. I knew I could give this baby something I never had. My heart was breaking.

When we arrived at the clinic we pulled into the small lot lined with a crowd of people holding signs protesting abortion. Afraid to look directly at their faces, I scanned the crowd in search of a path to the entrance. Terrified of eye contact, I tried to look down as I walked, but the protesters were loud, and my curiosity led me to look up. They seemed angry, and I was already feeling weak.

A Planned Parenthood representative came outside in an authoritative manner, and the protesters moved aside. She made her way towards me to offer me help through the madness.She braved this for me. I looked at my grandmother, and we got out. Stepping out and walking towards the entrance, the crowd moved in on me, shouting, "Don't kill your baby!" They waved their posters with images of tiny fetus parts, some bloody and deformed. We hurried to the front entrance.

One of the women shouting handed me a brochure, and I took it. I was curious. I didn't want to kill my baby. Of course, I didn't want to do this. They had no idea how I felt. I also wondered how many of these people would be willing to help me with the baby. My family wasn't willing; that's what they had essentially decided for me. I took the pamphlet and walked in with the escort.

The last thing I heard from the crowd was, "You don't have to do this! There's time to save your baby."

My baby. I *was* killing my baby.

The image of the bloody fetus was now in my mind. *What was I signing up for? How could I do this...kill my baby?*

I had to accept that I was going to hell if I made this choice. Over the years, I noticed the sign outside of the Catholic church I visited with my grandmother. "We are Pro-Life" which translated in my mind to "You will burn in hell if you choose otherwise." I shoved the images of flames and heat aside and picked up a *Seventeen* magazine. I began to flip through the pages, placing my focus on cute outfits and the beautiful girls who looked joyful and free. I felt sick; I wished I could feel that way.

Within minutes, my name was called, and I made my way to the back. The process began with an interview about my relationship with the father. The nurse asked if I had ever felt unsafe in my relationship. I wanted to be honest, but I didn't want to extend our time together, so I said, "No."

Next, we went into the exam room where I was given a robe to change into. The cold room and stiff robe felt harsh on my skin. I felt violated even though no one had entered the room. The nurse came in. She was friendly; her warmth made me immediately feel better. She completed an ultrasound on me. The nurse pointed to the tiny bean shape on the sonogram image. I was six weeks pregnant. This helped me to see that it didn't look like *my baby*, but this didn't change what this small miracle could grow into. I knew I was lying to myself, and that it would grow into a baby soon enough. I was more confused than ever. I was afraid to make the wrong choice. I heard the opinions of others as they weighed in on my future with and without a baby, but it didn't matter. I knew I'd have to deal with my own guilt as I lay in bed at night in the dark. I wondered if I could handle the heaviness of my choice.

I felt overwhelmed with all that I was facing: the chaos of my relationship with Robert, the truth about my own codependency and depression, and the images of bloody fetus parts on the protest signs. The things that sucked in my life were stacking. I couldn't imagine adding a living, breathing baby that needs love and stability into this equation. With tears in my eyes, I made my decision. It felt final. I knew what needed to be done.

The people in the parking lot began to fade from my mind, as I knew they wouldn't be taking care of me or keeping my baby safe.

The nurse went over the options for the procedure: to be awake or asleep. I chose to have twilight anesthesia, which meant they would be putting me slightly under, but I'd still be awake during it. I was afraid of the full anesthesia, and while I felt I deserved to die for this, I didn't want to. I felt selfish for wanting to keep myself awake and alive. I decided I was going to hell, for sure.

The day before my procedure, I decided to visit my mom. I lay on her sofa for hours, feeling the waves of nausea and guilt roll through me as I thought about what I was about to do. I wiped away tears and attempted to sleep. Finally, I decided to get up and reach for my diary, which was my refuge and friend through all of this. I found that I wrote the most when I was lost and feeling desperate, like I did in lockup. Sharing the thoughts with my diary that I was unwilling to say out loud helped. My mom turned *The Oprah Winfrey Show* on. I wasn't watching, but I couldn't help overhearing it as I wrote. The guest on the show snagged my attention. She was a bold and lively black woman who spoke with certainty about healing your life. She was courageous; her story pulled me in. Her name appeared on the TV screen: Iyanla Vanzant. I wrote her name down in my diary and continued to hang on her every word.

This woman spoke of being raped by a relative and her physically abusive ex-husband. There was something about her conviction; it was magnetic. She went on to explain her name change, graduation from law school, and essentially her rebirth. After all she had experienced, she still helped others to live their best lives. She mentioned her book called *One Day My Soul Just Opened Up*. I wrote the title down, knowing I needed to read this book. This woman sparked something in me; her journey reminded me that life wasn't over, even with all that had happened. I still had time to make things right, even if I did the unthinkable. That brave woman renewed a sense of hope in me. Her story reminded me I still had a chance for redemption. I didn't know when my life would shift or how my life would heal, but I now felt I had a chance. By the end of her interview, I saw my life, and myself, a little differently.

The morning I dreaded came, and I went through with it. The procedure was horrible; I hated the sounds as they used the machine to vacuum the fetus from my womb. I cried for days; I numbed myself with pain medication and the Xanax my aunt gave me. After the procedure, I expected to feel relieved. Instead, I felt empty and alone again.

CHAPTER 5

In the weeks that followed my procedure, my guilt was soothed by realizing Robert and I would have made horrible parents. I knew I made the right choice for me at the time. That was all that mattered. As my guilt faded, so did my love for Robert, or at least my desire to be with him. I didn't want to see him with another woman; I still cared for him, but I was tired of being abused. His anger made him unrecognizable. As he realized I was no longer interested, he began to pursue me. The more I avoided him, the more he pushed.

My friend Kelly and I were out at the movies and stopped in front of my house to smoke a joint before heading in. As we sat in her black Volkswagen, listening to Usher, and talking about the guy she was dating, Robert jumped on the hood of her car.

We both screamed!

Kelly beeped her horn repeatedly. She screamed at him, "Get off of my car you, asshole. I'm calling the police!" She was sassy, the kind of woman you couldn't quiet. She had never been around men who were physically abusive to women, and she wasn't afraid; she was appalled.

He looked at her, laughed, and then looked at me. His eyes were different. They were empty. I didn't recognize this man. Finally, he jumped off and ran.

I was terrified, I couldn't believe he was behaving this way so close to my home. I felt trapped by his behavior. I was stunned. Kelly was freaking out. "What the fuck was that? What just happened?"

I snapped out of it and said, "Let's go to the police station."

At the police station, I gave my statement to a familiar officer as he dispatched patrol to locate Robert. I remembered the last time I spoke to the police; I felt I was betraying a friend. This time around was much different. I didn't feel bad for Robert. I felt like I was protecting myself; I was genuinely worried. He looked like a mad man; I questioned his sanity. Within two hours Robert was arrested for violating his probation. I knew he'd be away for a few weeks; this bought me time to get my life together.

With a newfound urgency, I asked my grandmother to support me in getting my GED and my first car. I was desperate for a change. I knew I was headed in the wrong direction. I felt like this was my chance to make a change, and I had to take a chance to ask. She had recently retired and had some money. To my delight, she said, "Yes."

The fear that I felt drove me. I knew I had to act fast. An eighteen-year-old with an eighth-grade education wasn't going to get too far. My internal conflict of doubt and optimism led me into constant highs and lows. Part of me pushed forward and felt that anything was still possible. The other part of me was dark and heavy; she reminded of all my ugly memories that sparked insecurities. I fought to listen to the voice of optimism.

Two months had passed since Robert had gone to jail, and I was given the chance of a lifetime. A friend's sister offered to give me a opportunity; she was hiring for an administrative job at a financial institution. This position was reserved for college graduates or people with similar work experience, but she was willing to give me a chance. It felt like a miracle. She didn't care about my background; I told her I'd give it my best, and she believed me. I meant it. I saw my entire life transforming; I saw a way out.

With Robert away, it bought me time to focus on my own growth without his controlling ways. I felt free and happy. I was able to get in and out of my vehicle without the fear of him creeping up on me. The position opened up new doors for me, and I was introduced to different lifestyles beyond what I saw at home.

Our office was located in an affluent area known as the Main Line. It was an upper-class area compared to where I had been living for the past eighteen years. I felt slightly out of place as I attempted to hide all that I'd seen and experienced. I reminded myself I couldn't let anyone know about my past; I didn't want to scare anyone away. I'd go out to work outings and made some friends; the guys I got to know in the office revealed a different type of man to me: men who honored women and honored me. I also noticed how the women carried themselves. I had never spent time around professionals. It was an eye-opener; I now had people to look up to. All of this reminded me to do better.

CHAPTER 6

I felt my purse vibrate as I waited near the bar while I made small talk with a coworker. I was patiently waiting for my friend to return with my vodka cranberry. I couldn't wait to be twenty-one and not have to ask other adults for drinks. It was my office annual holiday party, and the ballroom was packed.

Everywhere I looked, a good time was being had. Everyone was smiling; my coworkers were so much more fun when drinking. The dance floor was filled with people singing along to Michael Jackson's "Pretty Young Thing," and the open bar was full familiar of smiling faces. I was one of them. *This is great,* I thought. I felt proud of myself; months had passed and I proved I was a valuable team member. When offered opportunities to go beyond what was expected, I challenged myself and signed up for the courses and passed the exams to get licensed in my field. I was able to see myself differently in that position. I was more inspired than ever, and I felt like life was going to keep getting better. For once, I felt like I was a part of something and creating a new identity. The party was at a fancy hotel in the King of Prussia Mall, so many of the team had rooms at the hotel so there was no holding back with the drinking.

My friend arrived with my bright red cocktail, and I thanked him and headed out to the hallway to check my phone.

Reaching into my purse, I felt the phone go off again. Feeling irritated by the urgency, I cursed the person who kept calling me repeatedly. *Who the hell is blowing up my phone?*

The cell phone screen lit up, displaying seven missed calls from a Philadelphia number. Worry swept over me. *Oh no! Did something happen to my family?*

The phone lit up again in my hand, startling me. I answered it, frustrated by the person on the other end for leading me to worry.

"Hello?"

"Nikki, it's me."

My heart skipped a beat. It was Robert; it had been months since I heard his voice. Startled, I took a big gulp of my cocktail.

"Nikki, hello? Are you there? I need to see you…"

He continued to talk. I took in his voice. He sounded gentle. I could hear the sadness in his voice. Something was different. Maybe it was the alcohol, but I wanted to hug him and help him, but I knew I couldn't.

I cut him short. "I have to go. Please leave me alone. I want both of us to be happy. I can't do this…"

He cut me off. "Nikki, please come see me. I want to see you. I'm staying with my sister in Center City. Come here tonight. I need you."

I sensed his emotion. He was going through something, but it wasn't my problem.

"I can't, Robert. I'm at my work party in King of Prussia."

"You're halfway here. Come down after," he said.

I hoped we could one day be friends, but it was too soon to hang out. His sadness didn't necessarily mean he healed.

"Another time, Robert. I gotta go. My boss is calling us in for dinner." That was a lie, but I had to get off the phone. I hung up and headed straight for the bar.

Even though I felt sad, I felt empowered by my strength to stay away and protect myself. I knew I was getting stronger each day.

The party was winding down, and I was texting my friends to find out what was going on closer to home. The usual party spots were happening, so I decided to head to a friend's place, which was a forty-minute drive from the holiday work party. I had my new black Acura CL V6, and it was brand new and fast. I loved driving it. It was winter and cold outside, but the alcohol lit a fire in me, and I was ready to party.

About an hour later, I finally made it to Dena's place. Her house sat on a wooded lot, back a bit from the narrow country road. Her driveway was filled with other cars, and when I pulled up, I saw my friend, Matt, getting out of the car in front of me. Dena was there, too. She was standing in the driveway with two six-packs of Coors Light in her hands, greeting everyone as they pulled in. A few of my friends, including Dena, rented this home in the woods as an upgraded party space with lots of room to watch sports, drink, and smoke. On this particular night, there were more people there than usual.

As I stepped out of my car, I reached into the back for my purse, and I saw the look on Dena's face change. She looked spooked. I turned to see what had caught her eye, and I saw a small, gold car parked with the headlights on and Robert walking up the driveway toward me.

Since he didn't have a car, it hit me that he must have stolen his sister's car. She wouldn't just let him take it that far, especially with his recent history. His sister was a sensible, successful pharmacist who was married and living a respectable life with her husband in the city.

When Robert got to my car, his eyes were wide, and he had the possessed look that I had become familiar with by then. I was afraid. I had hoped that Matt or the other guys inside would come out to help, but most of the men I hung out with were afraid of Robert. Dena rushed over to talk some sense into Robert, but she couldn't do much. I instantly regretted that I didn't go down to his sister's, and I wished I had been nicer to him on the phone. I somehow managed to blame myself.

Robert grabbed my arm; I could see his eyes were distant, as if he left his body. He snapped at me, "You're coming with me. Tell your friends goodbye."

I pulled away, but he gripped me tighter. He dragged me over to the car and pushed me in. Then he jumped in the car too and backed out of the driveway. As we pulled out and saw Matt and Dena yelling and coming down the driveway toward us, I knew it was too late; their screams were pointless.

As soon as we reached the road, Robert shifted the car in drive and punched me in the face. "You didn't want to come see me? You want to be a bitch?" He hit me again; this time I felt the blood dripping down from my nose. I had on a brand new Armani Exchange jacket, and though it was red, I could still see the dark red stain from my blood. He hit me on the head again, and I saw a bright light after the blow. He hit me so hard I was surprised I didn't black out. I tried to open the door and jump out of the moving car, but he wouldn't let go of my arm. I was trapped, and yet I didn't stop trying. I noticed car lights behind us in the distance, and I thought maybe it was Matt. I knew Matt wasn't the typical alpha male, but I hoped he might step up and surprise me tonight. I needed him.

When the car door shut, he punched me once again. He told me, "You thought you were better than me? Your ass is fucking dead." He was maniacal. I knew he was right, and in that moment I thought about my Grandmom, I thought about her lying in bed peacefully and how she'd have to hear about what happened to me when I didn't come home. This thought hurt me. I realized I didn't have a lot of reasons to live, but I didn't want to die. I was falling deeper into the acceptance of my fate as we sped down the dark, narrow roads as he took his anger out on me with blows to my body and head. Covering my head the best I could, I wondered how many more hits I could handle. All I could taste was my blood in my mouth. I realized I was lost, and I didn't recognize where we were. We were driving alongside a field. The more my grandmother came to mind and the more I dealt with the idea of her broken heart, the more I knew I had to talk him down. So, then I lied and pleaded with him to give me one more chance. I told him I was wrong about us and that I wanted to have one more chance to make it up to him. He was still hitting me every minute or so, and I covered my face so his blows crushed my arm. My body was weary, but my spirit kept fighting to go on. He was so tall, and his long arms allowed him to choke me and hold me against the passenger's window as he drove. He eventually let off a bit, and every moment I could, I repeated how sorry I was. I told him how much I loved him. Eventually he pulled off the road into an empty field. It was mid-December, and the ground was frozen, and the corn crops that lined these fields during the summer were now cut down. The night was clear, and yet I could only see what the faint moonlight allowed. I thought, *This is it. This is where I am going to die. He's going to leave me out here until someone finds me.*

He got out and walked to the back of the car. I thought he'd grab something out of the trunk, but he didn't. He continued to my door, opened it, and said, "Get into the back seat now."

I knew my time was growing near; he was going to kill me. I wondered how he was going to kill me in the back seat. Suddenly, there was a shift. I felt empty, and I had emotionally given up on being saved. In the backseat, there was a strange calm. He told me to bend over, and I followed his order. Surprisingly, he pulled up my dress and pushed himself inside of me. Everything inside of me felt dead. I did everything I could to emotionally tune out and leave my body until he finished, if he didn't kill me before then.

His grunting and animalistic movements disgusted me. I felt like a stranger was having sex with me.

After he finished, something seemed different. The rage wasn't there anymore, and he looked more disgusted than angry. More importantly, he wasn't violent anymore. I continued to apologize and beg for one more chance to make this up to him. Again, I lied to save my life, but I hated him with every fiber of my being in that moment. How could anyone want to have sex after beating me like he did? I was a bloody mess. I didn't dare look in the mirror. I only saw the blood all over my clothing and my lips were broken and puffy. But he wanted to destroy me, and I couldn't do anything to stop him. I thought, *Is this rape?* No, he was my ex-boyfriend; I had willingly had sex with him in the past. Still, I felt uncomfortable about it, and I didn't want it. This wasn't typical sex. I had no choice in it, and it felt dirty and gross. Still, I couldn't be sure about what had just happened. I was sure of one thing though: he had worse problems than I had ever imagined.

Once he got back in the driver's seat, I asked him to take me to his sister's place. I explained that we could hide out there until I was better. He looked at me. I could tell he was deciding whether or not to take me there. Without a word, he started the car and drove off. We started our drive to Philadelphia. On the way home, I began to make plans with him. I led him to believe I was in this thing for real. I wasn't leaving him. I had developed the ability to influence other people into action; it was one of the survival skills I learned as a child. I had to figure out how to get what I wanted while staying safe in tough times. I developed this skill through dealing with my parents when they weren't coherent. I kept up the game during our drive, and though it was working, I could see the worry on his face. As we approached the city, we were driving alongside beautifully lit waterfront structures along Boathouse Row, and I knew we were close to his sister's place. The freeway lights were brighter on this stretch of the freeway, and as I looked out of the passenger side window, I caught a reflection of my face from the bright lights. I didn't recognize myself. I was more swollen than I had realized. I wondered if I were okay. Did I have a concussion? The sky was even brighter as we pulled onto South Street. The sun was going to rise soon, and instead of taking me to his sister's, he decided to drop me off at the hospital down the street from his sister's house. I promised I wouldn't tell on him. As he pulled off, my legs fell out from beneath me.

CHAPTER 7

I struggled to stand up, feeling weaker than I ever had. Still in disbelief that I made it out alive, I realized how disoriented I was as I gazed at the ER entrance. I gathered my strength to make it to the door, and as I began walking, a man exiting saw me and hurried over.

"Who did this to you?" He called for help. "Security, call the police! She needs help out here."

Another man and a woman rushed over to help me into a wheelchair and wheeled me into the hospital. As I was ushered through the emergency room and into triage, I did my best to avoid the eyes of people we passed.

I was alive, and Robert didn't kill me. Everything else in life seemed irrelevant.

The nurse walked into the room with an intensity that led me to believe she hadn't lived the easiest life herself. She handed me a cup of water and pain medication. I was trying to take a sip from my paper cup of water, but my lips were too swollen. She seemed to soften a bit as she spoke to me, "Do you know the person who did this to you?"

I flashed back to me begging for my life in the car. I promised not to tell. He must've believed me, and that's why I was still breathing. I felt like I owed him.

On the other hand, I knew I had to tell or else I may end up dead. He wasn't well. He needed help.

Before I could speak, two police officers walked into the room. I glanced at their guns, and I felt a bit safer. I told them everything. I was too numb to cry. I was alive, but I barely felt like it. I had to go to the bathroom, but the nurse prepared me for the exam the Doctor would perform, she mentioned a rape kit and collecting evidence.

Rape. The word cut through me, making me feel like a fraud. I felt like a liar. He didn't rape me. He was my ex-boyfriend. Rape kits were for women who were really raped—by strangers. I didn't know what that was, but did they have to call it rape?

"But I don't know if it was rape. Do I have to do this exam? I'm not sure I want to press charges for sex."

The female officer signaled her male counterpart to give us a moment. When he stepped outside, she sat beside me as if we had known each other for some time.

"Ms. Sylvester, did he penetrate you?"

I was relieved by the simplicity of her question. "Yes."

"Did you want him to?" She looked at me, waiting for a response.

"No, not tonight, but I did before, and I didn't stop him tonight."

She cut me short. "That doesn't matter. He took you from your car, hurt you, and then entered you. That is rape. That's far from consensual sex."

I heard what she was saying, but I didn't fully believe her at the time. We continued with the process, and I held my pee until my bladder couldn't take it any longer. I was afraid to go into a bathroom alone; I was scared to see myself. I could feel how ugly I looked.

As I debated going into the bathroom, my anxiety began to grow. I was shaking and feeling like I couldn't breathe suddenly. The doctor gave me an injection that quieted the noise of what I had just lived through.

Finally, I calmed down and made it into the bathroom. I looked at my swollen face in the mirror, I didn't recognize myself. The whites in my eyes had turned red, the bridge of my nose was swollen and wide, and blood had formed scabs around my nostrils. My nose was fractured, but thankfully it was not broken. I wondered if my nose would ever look the same. My cheekbones resembled a boxer who barely managed to make it twelve rounds. My lips had tripled in size; I felt like an alien. Unrecognizable. *Who would want to have sex with this?* I felt disgusting; the thought of someone having that urge made me feel nauseous. As I gazed at myself in the hospital mirror under the bright institutional lighting, my medicine began to kick in, and relief came with it. I knew I would be needing some of it at home. Within three hours, I had cooperated with the police, finished all the exams and the paperwork, and my grandmother picked me up to take me home. No matter what was happening in my life, my Grandmom, Dolly, was a safe person for me. I was comforted by her nurturing presence amidst all the strange faces. As we moved through the hospital to the parking garage, I felt my paranoia slice through the high from my pain pills. The fear became the loudest as we reached the exit. Security was by our side, but still I felt Robert could run out from anywhere and attempt to finish me off.

When my grandmother and I pulled up to my home, the local police were waiting in the driveway. This duo was familiar with my violent history with Robert.

My grandmother invited them in with us so we could move into the warmth of home. The two sat down on the sofa, and I sat in the La-Z-Boy recliner. I wanted to tuck my face behind a blanket and have my grandmother handle this for me, but I reminded myself that as police officers, they'd seen worse.

"We don't have the best news for you. Robert hasn't been located. We've been to his parents' place, his sister's as well. No one has spoken to him; he still has his sister's car."

I suddenly felt more vulnerable. He could be watching us right now. I shifted in my seat. "What should I do? I'm scared he may come here."

Looking at my grandmother, I could tell she was concerned. I wished the police could sit outside in their cars. That would be the only way I'd ever rest at all here.

"Do you have somewhere else you could stay?" The officer

continued, "A place he has never been to or someone he doesn't know is best."

My body felt unsafe; my world was fragile. As I thought of where I could stay safely, my mind was interrupting with graphic images of horror. I imagined Robert regretting his decision to let me go and deciding that he wanted me dead.

My mind raced for people and places. Who would want me, looking like this, to stay? I was hideous. Not to mention this person had to be brave. I was hiding from someone who wanted me dead just hours ago. I pulled out my phone. I browsed the missed calls and texts from friends who were at the party I was taken from. I would figure it out.

CHAPTER 8

The alarm went off, and I couldn't move. My body was heavy, and the cool air on my face was uninviting, signaling the rest of my body tucked under the cover to stay put. I watched the clock as the minutes passed. As the numbers changed, my body seemed to become heavier. The thought of getting dressed, driving thirty-five minutes to work, and speaking to another human seemed unmanageable. I wanted to erase everything and hide from everything. My boss was kind enough to let me stay with her until Robert was found, which made it harder for me to call out from work. She had done so much for me. I owed it to her. I knew I needed to pull it together.

I had already exceeded my sick and vacation time by two weeks at this juncture. My hand fumbled for the phone on the bedside table, knocking over my prescription bottle and the remote. I lifted the phone and dialed my office.

"I'm sorry. I'm really sick. I can't come in today." My own guilt seemed to stab me as the excuse left my mouth. I wasn't sick. I wasn't coughing or vomiting, but I was far from well. As I listened to my boss warn me about calling off again for the tenth time, the tears streamed down my face. I hung up the phone. I knew I was throwing my life away day by day, but I didn't know how to stop. I didn't know how to feel better.

Nearly two months had passed since Robert was arrested. This time he wasn't coming home for years, which relieved me as much as it hurt me. I hated that he couldn't just let me be and live his life. Instead he hurt us both. I was in deep resistance. I also shamed myself for caring, for feeling this way.

This job was the best thing that ever happened to me, and I was ruining it. *Typical me*, I thought. I fought back against the voices in my head. I was at war with myself. *I can't live like this anymore. I cannot.* The tears turned to sobbing, and I jumped out of bed, afraid of what I was feeling. I threw on my jacket and headed to my doctor's office. I didn't care that I didn't have an appointment; I knew they would see me before the day was over. I couldn't be alone with myself anymore. I had never felt so in the dark, I felt empty and scared. I needed help.

Three hours later, I found myself sitting in the private room, nervous yet somewhat relieved. *Today is the day I am going to feel better,* I told myself as I thumbed through the women's health magazine.

The door opened, and Dr. Getty walked in with his warm smile.

"How are you doing, young lady? It's been awhile. What brings you in?"

I could feel my throat tighten. "I don't know what's wrong with me, but I'm scared."

His eyes softened. "Can you explain what you are feeling exactly?"

"I don't want to live like this anymore..." I cracked. I broke down. The tears streamed as I sobbed the details of my life out between breaths.

That was the first time I had cried to someone since I was a child. I had been taught it was weak to cry so I held back from showing emotion. He listened as I went on about my family, Robert, lockup, and now work struggles.

His eyes told me he knew all about it. His understanding soothed my sadness. This doctor had treated my parents since I was born; he helped my Dad get clean. He knew what I was working through.

Handing me another tissue, he continued, "Nikki, you've got to get off those pills. I know Xanax helps with anxiety, but it's not good long term. They are depressants, and now, well, you are depressed. I would like you to try a long-term treatment plan. How about you try anti-depressants and some lifestyle changes? Let's see how it goes."

I expressed my fears about taking antidepressants. I didn't want to be known as the emotional woman who needs meds to be normal. There was definitely a stigma, and I didn't want to be a part of it. He placed his hand on my shoulder as I wiped the tears from cheeks and said, "Nikki, let go of the labels and focus on quality of life now. If this helps you, it's worth it. You're suffering right now, and you don't need to. This isn't a forever plan; it's a get better plan."

He was right that I was suffering. Life didn't have to feel this way. He prescribed me Paxil, and I walked out feeling something I hadn't felt for a while: hope.

The feeling I had walking to my car that day was short-lived. I tried my best to get back to myself, the ambitious Nikki who had big plans for her career. I couldn't find her; she was gone. Within a few weeks, I had lost my job and found myself in a deeper despair without any direction. I watched myself ruin the best thing to ever happen to me. My way out was a burned bridge, and I lit the match. For the rest of the winter, I was in my bed in my grandmother's home, and I didn't want to be bothered. I was in hibernation. I just hoped I would make it back out. But for the moment, I knew I wasn't ready to deal with the real world. Not yet.

CHAPTER 9

Reaching into my duffle bag in the passenger seat, I unzipped it, ruffling through the lingerie and heels to find the pint of vodka I brought from my mom's freezer. I took a long swig and chased the vodka with a warm Sprite I had left in the car all day. The alcohol warmed me as it traveled down and settled in my belly. With each sip, I felt my fear fade a bit. I took one more big pull from the bottle to ensure I had the courage to do this.

I pulled down my visor once more to see myself in the mirror. *Not bad*, I thought I as examined my face. I decided more eyeliner would help; I added another layer of lip gloss and reminded myself that I had no other choice. This had to work, and it would.

As I approached the entrance of the club, the security guards watched me as I moved closer.

"ID please," the taller guard requested.

"Okay, I am here to audition. I spoke to Sal earlier; he's expecting me."

The guard pulled out this walkie-talkie and called for Sal.

I stood there awkwardly, feeling like I was already naked. *Fuck, I should've had another shot.* I stared out into the street to avoid eye contact with the guards. *Come on, Sal, let's get this over with,* I thought as I did my best to appear confident and sexy.

Two minutes later, the short, round, balding, Italian man came to the entrance to walk me in. Sal guided me through the hall with dim blue lighting and opened a door to his office.

"So, Nikki, have you done this before?"

"No, but I know I can."

He spoke as he sorted through paperwork on his desk, "We'll see. I'll be the judge of that. Let's get you on stage and see how you do."

My heart was racing. I wanted him to like me; I wanted to be good at this. Hell, I needed to be good at this. It had been two months since I quit my job due to panic attacks, and I was behind on everything. I couldn't handle a job where I had to stay sober, not now. The urgency lit a fire in me. "I'll do good. Let's do it."

He looked up, and I could sense he was curious about me. "Alright then. What's your stage name for tonight?"

Oh fuck, that's right. I need a name. My mind quickly scanned for sexy names. "Giselle"

The door opened and a tall, beautiful brunette walked into the office. She had a silver bikini on. She was older; perhaps she was in her late thirties. I could tell she'd been doing this for a while.

Sal perked up a bit. "Vanity, this is Giselle. She's auditioning. Take her back to get dressed, and let's see what she's got."

She turned to me, looking me up and down. She looked unimpressed, which didn't help matters, but I was focused. This had quickly become a life-or-death situation, at least in the smallness of my world. I had to pull myself out of the hole I dug and fast. She turned around. "Follow me," she said.

I walked behind her as she led me through the hall and into the club. I watched the women dancing on the three stages. They looked mysterious under the lighting. Their moves were sexy, and they were a lot more flexible than I was. I felt silly thinking about myself practicing in my mirror at home; I definitely didn't look like that.

Vanity walked to the back corner of the club and opened a door, waiting for me to catch up. "Let's go, chica! You gotta get dressed."

The brightly lit room was narrow and lined with mirrors and stools for the ladies to get dressed. The women were getting dressed, doing their hair and makeup, while complaining about men. I felt out of place as I walked to the back for the open stool. Women were naked, having conversations with each other. I felt uncomfortable already. I pulled out my newly purchased clear platform heels and a black-lace, string-bikini top and black booty shorts to wear over a g-string.

Looking in the mirror, I desperately wished my boobs were larger for this. I found myself checking out the women in the reflection, and I felt like a little girl next to some of these voluptuous women. Reaching back into my bag, I opened the bottle to my Xanax, broke off a small piece, and placed it under my tongue to ease my nerves.

"Giselle, you're on stage in fifteen minutes. Get out here and sit at the bar. Watch the other girls so you know what you're doing," Vanity yelled from the door.

Staring at myself in the mirror, my mind raced as the women next to me argued over a customer. *How the hell did I end up here? I was doing so well. Now I am here about to showcase my nearly naked body in front of strange men.* I interrupted that train of thought, soothing myself as I made my way out to the stage with a gentle reminder that this would only be temporary.

As I sat at the bar, my bare skin touching the leather barstool, I gazed at the women seductively moving on the stage. Their looks were intimidating. I wondered if I could look half as sexy. If so, that would be good enough, I decided. I repeated again, *This is only temporary.*

My mind drifted from the dancers to my plot to get rich quick and move out of Pennsylvania. A fresh start in warmer weather was inviting; it felt safe and secure. I knew I could put my past behind me if only I could escape. These visions fueled me; I was ready to get this done. I could tell the Xanax had begun to kick in. I was no longer nervous.

The DJ cut through the music with his announcement. "Welcome to the stage, this pretty young thing, Gisellllle." He stretched out my new stage name as if he were announcing a boxing match.

I took a deep breath, walked up the few stairs, and took my place on the stage to the left. Beyoncé and Sean Paul blared as I allowed myself to get lost in the music. The men posted up at the bar faded from my awareness. I didn't have to be flexible or a dancer; I only had to be sexy, so I slowly moved my body to the music, worked the floor, and twirled teasingly around the pole. I danced with myself and for myself. I needed to make money and fast.

The song ended, and I came back to reality. I stepped off the stage, and Sal was waiting for me. He smiled. "Come fill out your paperwork. Let's get you on the schedule."

This felt like the only sort of job I could handle. The only problem was that I hated men at the time. Still, it was the only option I could see for quick money with no need to keep it together. I was a mess, but so were most of the women on the roster.

Two weeks into the gig, and I had a regular customer. This made my work easy. I had one person as the source of almost all the money I made.

"Hey girl, you've got a delivery." Junior, my favorite security, greeted me as I walked into the club. I liked Junior because he was a nice guy. He respected me as if I were a sister rather than someone he wanted to make a move on. I can assure you this was rare in the club I worked in.

I smiled. "Is it a new Mercedes?" I asked jokingly. "Can we take it to the car now so I don't forget it tonight?" Junior grabbed the box from inside and walked it to my trunk. I was grateful for him. Not just for helping me with the gift but for watching my back since I'd arrived.

The guards walked us in and out of the club to ensure us dancers were safe. While most of our customers were cool, there were episodes.

My favorite customer was Larry, an introverted, divorced older, white businessman. He was in mergers and acquisitions and took great care of me. The thing I liked most about him was that he didn't want me to dance for him, he wanted me to talk to him and keep him company. He also liked privacy, so he reserved time in the VIP rooms and bought me the champagne I liked and I got drunk and talked with him for hours. While we were talking, he'd ask me what I needed. I'd tell him everything from money, purses to electronics. He'd leave the packages here at the club and the guards would get them into my car.

If it weren't for Larry, I would have been broke. I was a horrible stripper. I felt like a beggar asking a man if I could dance for him. Luckily, I met a regular within days of starting or else I would've been screwed. Larry came in specifically for me, and he made sure my financial needs were met and then some. Aside from Larry, I went on stage for my required songs and then went to the bar to drink and chat with men who seemed like we may be friends outside of the club. When attractive men came in the club, I immediately wished I wasn't wearing a fishnet outfit and clear heels. I felt ashamed, but not ashamed enough to quit and find a regular job.

I had been able to get over my stage fright, but I was horrible at making money in the club because I didn't want to be touched. I also didn't want to touch men. Touching was supposedly prohibited, but that couldn't be further from the truth. Men pushed boundaries, and some women welcomed it. I wasn't one of them, and, therefore, I was "no fun," as one man reminded me as I pushed his hand off my ass.

After enough drinks, I was able to work the crowd, noticing which men were into me from the stage. I felt so ridiculous asking a man if he wanted to a dance; I hated to be rejected, and if he said yes, I barely wanted to dance for him. Lose/lose for me. Most nights, I made under $200 because I preferred talking to men as if they were my friends. I was horrible at the hustle. I admired the women in the club who worked the room and made sure they got money from everyone. These women would say what they needed to say and get what they wanted, even if that meant the men simply handing them a twenty-dollar bill to get them to move on. No shame in their game; this was all business to them. I envied their hustle.

For me, this was an intimate experience that would take time to lead up to. I numbed myself to let down my guard and become freer. I had only been with a handful of men, and here I was exposing myself in this way. It didn't feel safe to me, physically or emotionally. It took me time to warm up to men as it was, and after what happened with Robert, I was sensitive. The alcohol was my liquid courage, but it made me tired. At the end of the night, some friends would be headed to an after-hours club, and I felt I could barely make it home. That night everything changed.

"Girl, you coming out with us, right?" Jazmine had her hands on my shoulders as I sat on the barstool, chugging a Red Bull. The night was ending. Now I needed to wake up from my numb state.

"I am so tired. I can't," I said.

Mark, one of our regulars, overheard us talking and jumped in, "Giselle, you better come out. You're not driving home yet anyway.

You're in no state to drive."

I took another sip of the can. I knew he was right. I wanted my pj's right now. *Maybe I'll sleep in the car,* I thought. Just as I thought about napping in my car, Jazmine moved beside me and whispered in my ear, "Come into the bathroom. I have something for you."

I perked up and turned to look at her face. She looked mischievous. I finished my drink in one final gulp and got up to follow her.

In the bathroom, she locked the door. I wondered if she was about to make her move on me. I had kissed women, but I wasn't down for all of that right now.

"Keep this to yourself, cool?"

"Of course, Jaz," I replied. "What is it?"

She reached into her bedazzled bra and pulled out a small white bag. "Go into the bathroom and use your nail to snort some of this. You'll be perfect after."

"Coke?"

"Yeah, trust me. Try it," she urged. She didn't realize she didn't have to urge me too hard. I had tried cocaine with my older cousin a few times, but I had always been anxious so I didn't like it. This time was different; I needed something to speed me up.

She unlocked the door as I went into the stall alone. I sat down on the toilet as if I were going to pee in case the other girls came in. I dipped my French-manicured, acrylic nail into the bag and lifted a tiny mound of the white powder out of the small ziploc bag. I looked at it and sniffed it up my nose with a long inhale.

Within seconds, I felt the powder fall into my throat and the tingling sensation woke me up. I decided to do one more line to ensure I'd be awake. I stood up, adjusted myself, wiped my nose, and walked out of that bathroom like a new woman. Now I was ready to go out. The cocaine was like a medicine; I couldn't remember the last time I felt so alive. "Alright, I'm in. Let me get changed." Jaz and Mark smiled in response and shooed me to the dressing room. I felt a rush of energy as I changed into my jeans and top. We moved from club to club and finally to one that was after hours where they served alcohol beyond the legal serving times for Pennsylvania. We partied until the sun came up. Every thirty minutes, we were in the bathroom getting our fix, and I was obsessed. I could've stayed up another day doing lines and drinking cocktails, but we ran out and eventually so did my energy.

This was the beginning of my love for cocaine. The white powder had me wired. I could drink for hours and hours yet still function. This changed the way I worked in the club. I was chattier when I was high as the drug opened me up, and I let down my guard with men more. In the coming weeks, I reconnected with old friends who I used to party with, and getting high would happen whether I was working or not. My habit was becoming expensive, and I had no plan to stop.

Everything changed the night I met Warren. I was on stage when I noticed someone I hadn't seen before. He caught my attention because he was more attractive than the men who frequented the club. When my song ended, I made my way off the stage and went directly over to him and his friend.

The first thing I noticed was that he wasn't thirsty for attention from women. I could tell he got plenty of that, but he was just here with his boy drinking and the vibe was different. There was something about him that had me intrigued. He was sexy, the fit of his clothing revealed his muscular build. Deep olive complexion, wavy dark hair, and strong jawline. But it was more than the physical, I felt I needed to know him.

With a curious smile on his face, he asked, "So what's your story?"

I took a seat at the bar next to him, wondering which version to tell.

CHAPTER 10

I was intimidated by Warren, yet intrigued. He was mysterious. He was in and out of Pennsylvania as he flew home to the West Coast for his business. I was intrigued by the lifestyle that allowed such freedom, yet this also intimidated me because he was unlike my friends and myself. He didn't get high nor did he need to get drunk; he maintained control of himself.

Over the next few weeks, Warren and I began to see each other more frequently when he was in town. Our casual dating consisted of dinners and sleeping at his hotel. I didn't know too much about him. Our relationship wasn't deep, but it was a much-needed refuge from my crazy life. That's all I needed at the time. When I was with him, I couldn't openly get high and stay up all night. I'd sneak into the restroom to give myself some life with a bump every so often, but I had to be discreet about it. I went into the club less and less, which felt good even though my money was dwindling.

Every few weeks, Warren's cousin would come back east to work with him. That's when we'd go out and party in the city. I invited my girlfriends to join us. One particular night, we all hit the diner for breakfast, and we were headed to my place to drop off my friends. As we turned onto my street, I could feel I wasn't ready to sleep. I wanted to stay up and party. I wasn't sure how Warren would feel about my change of heart.

The idea of continuing the party was more enticing than heading home to have sex and sleep. I was wired from the lines I had snuck in throughout the night. I knew I couldn't sleep; I wanted more.

Softening my voice, as if I was suddenly tired, I said, "You know what? I think it's best I stay home with the girls tonight, so they're comfortable here."

Warren turned to face me. His dark brown eyes were relaxed. "That's cool. We'll link up later this week."

I smiled, feeling free and secretly ready for another cocktail.

We pulled up in front of my place at two thirty a.m., and the driveway was full of cars. Every light in the small, ranch-style home was turned on. My roommates at the time were two guys from high school who worked through the week, but once Friday came around, they typically partied all the way through the weekend until Sunday morning.

"Damn, what's going on here?"

"It looks like we've found the after-party," I responded to Warren, wondering what he was thinking. It was pretty damn obvious. I continued, "My roommates like to let loose on the weekends. They won't be sleeping much."

"Why's that?"

I paused, wondering if I should tell the truth.

"Powder."

"Everyone in there does powder?" Warren looked at me with a slight smirk.

Dammit, he's totally judging me now. Regretting what I said, I responded, "Yep, pretty much."

My girlfriends emptied out of his car, and I remained to tell him goodbye, but I got much more than that.

The quiet of the inside of his Chrysler sedan felt awkward. He stared at the house with a surprised look on his face. Worried, I figured my facade was up; he knew I was high, too.

"Why didn't you tell me about your roommates? I thought they were squares. I didn't know they get down like this."

I was confused by his tone. I wondered if he were also down for the party. I didn't get it.

"I didn't want to showcase the activities at my place. Why? Do you get high, too?"

He shot back, "Fuck no. But you know my logistics business?"

I nodded and listened as he continued. "I'm in *this* business. We have a little operation going." He signaled to the home as he referred to the people getting high.

It suddenly made sense. I didn't pry into his life because I didn't want him prying into mine. But now I was even more curious. How did he get it back from the West Coast? Suddenly I was hit with questions I wanted to ask, but I refrained and instead listened.

Warren relaxed in the driver seat as he prepared for the proposition. "There's an opportunity for you here. I don't work with small stuff like what's happening here. But you could."

I perked up. I knew nothing about selling cocaine. I only consumed it, but I knew we bought a lot, and the idea of making money excited me.

"I'm down." He smiled back. This felt dangerous, and suddenly our casual dynamic became much more thrilling. Now I was reconsidering sex.

"Alright, you know this could work out nicely for you." We sat for a moment in silence. The windows had fogged up, and the car was still running.

I considered the bit of money I had left in my account. I hoped it wasn't out of my budget. I didn't want to disclose how broke I was, but if I had to, I would. "Wait, how much would it cost to start?"

"I got you. I'll help you get started."

The next time Warren and I got together, it was all about business. He taught me a few things about the business and spotted me a half-ounce to get started. I shifted from consumer to dealer, and suddenly I was in high demand amongst my friends. The half-ounce was gone in no time.

Two days later, I was back with Warren for the re-up. I exchanged the money for double the product. This relationship now met so many needs: I was making money, getting the attention I craved from a man, and now I had a free supply of my drug of choice. It wasn't free because I did the supply; it was free because I sold bags to friends, and they shared with me.

The more people who bought, the more they would do it with me, too. Most nights I didn't have to leave my house; my roommates and their friends were steady customers.

When they pressured me to share with them or break some out for free, I was able to tell them, "Sorry, it's not mine." They got it; they knew a man was giving this to me, and they weren't trying to have trouble with him. That was enough. They would instead buy some, instantly pour out some of the white powder on the nearest table, and proceed to divide it up into tiny white lines. One would be for me.

Between the nearly constant high and the perceived power, I was hooked. People needed what I had. Plus, men respected me; it was much different than dancing. I was done with Giselle; she was dead.

Now that I was fully aware of Warren's operation, our conversations shifted, and he invited me to Atlantic City where I discovered the act of money laundering. To me, we were just having fun. I watched him gamble as we posted up at various blackjack tables at the nicest casino in Atlantic City. I grew up in the casinos with my parents as they both gambled. For them, it was a potential way out. This gambling trip was different. I was now twenty-one, and I could partake in all the adult fun. I wouldn't use my fake ID in the casino; the security was strict and not worth the hassle.

As Warren doubled down and made his bets, I ordered cocktails from the waitress each time she passed by. I'd pass her a five dollar casino chip and slip off into the bathroom to do a bump. This was my recipe for all-night drinking. At the end of the night, he'd exchange tens of thousands of dollars of chips into the cashier for cash. Now the money was gambling earnings, not drug income. This lifestyle was a gamble in itself, I knew I was playing with fire, but it kept me warm.

As exciting as my adventures with Warren were, it was short-lived. Yet the lessons I learned would come in handy where I was headed.

CHAPTER 11

The day after my twenty-second birthday, I was still hungover as I pulled up to our hotel on the Las Vegas Strip. I was enchanted by the bright, flashing lights and the possibilities. The taxi driver stopped at the entrance of our hotel. I took in the scenery as I made my way through the small lobby. It was far from what I expected. Turned off by the carnival decor and smoky interior, I reminded myself that it was free, and I could leave as soon as I changed my clothes.

As I reached the casino floor, I spotted my friend Jake and two of his friends I recognized from high school. With drinks in their hands and excitement on their faces, I could tell it would be an intense three days.

We exchanged hugs and hellos and headed straight for the bar to do shots. "Nikki! You ready for Vegas?" As I braced myself for the vodka shots being poured, Jake reached into his pocket, pulled out a small bag, and handed it to me discretely. "Look what I brought."

I recognized that it was ecstasy right away and thought, *Oh, shit.*

"You guys came prepared!"

We held up our shots. "What happens in Vegas... You know the fucking rest!"

From that point on the party did not stop, except when we slept, which was minimal. This was fine by me. I wanted to get fucked up and have the time of my life. We went to the room to change and soon connected with the other six guys who were in the group. The group had this Vegas trip planned for months. Jake and I had been close for years, and he invited me two weeks prior when he realized my birthday was approaching. The boys were here for a conference, and I was the only female who decided to brave the masculinity. It didn't matter because after working in the club, I could deal with this harmless crew. I was used to being the lone female in a group of men.

We roamed the strip as a group, stopping at the tourist spots for beers poured in plastic guitar cups. By the time we made it to the female pirate show on the sidewalk, I was done sightseeing.

I nudged Jake. "I'm over walking. Let's go out. I have some powder. You have the pills, right?"

He smiled. "Yep."

We said goodbye to the group and hopped in the taxi line. As we stood in line, he handed me half a yellow pill. I swallowed it down with my mega-sized Grey Goose and Redbull and wondered what was to come of the night. As we traveled in the taxi, I pulled out my small bag of cocaine, lifted some out with my nail, and inhaled the white powder. Jake looked over, and I got some out for him. He also inhaled the bump right off my nail. My long acrylic nails came in handy for my habits. I felt the rush of the powder move through me as the taxi pulled up to the bright green hotel: the MGM.

Our taxi driver suggested Studio 54, so there we were. As the two of us waited in line, I felt my body begin to tingle. I felt a chill and realized the pill was hitting me. I latched onto Jake's arm and asked him how he was feeling. "Wonderful...just wonderful," he murmured, but his eyes told me differently.

"Are you sure?"

He nodded and smiled. "You know me, Nik. I'm ready to party."

I wondered how long he had been drinking before I arrived. Fifteen minutes later, we had moved through the long line and into the dark nightclub. As we scanned for the nearest bar, a woman who appeared to be wearing nothing but glitter swung across the top of the nightclub, hanging on a trapeze.

"Wow, we are definitely not in Philly anymore," Jake said and I stood silently, mesmerized as two more women swung and swirled like beautiful, aerial acrobats. I couldn't tell if the show was really this incredible or it was just the ecstasy. It didn't matter at this point.

Before the show ended, Jake abruptly walked off.

"Jake!"

I followed him, yelling for him, and then he looked backed and signaled with his hand to wait.

Jeez, okay, then. I felt his energy dampen mine, so instead of standing there awkwardly in the middle of the dance floor, I decided to head over to the bar. As I made my way over, I danced with the crowd and felt my energy surge once more, and I was back to myself and ready to party.

Upon reaching the bar, I stood at the edge of the crown of people, waiting for drinks. I was in between a couple and a woman standing alone, just like I was. The couple was grinding all over one another, and I could tell they'd be having amazing sex in just a few hours. Suddenly, I felt like a creep for watching them, and I decided to strike up a conversation with the woman by my side.

"Did your friend run off to the restroom, too?"

I was relieved when she smiled back. "No, but I feel you! My friends are around here somewhere; I decided to get a drink before joining them."

We continued to make small talk until we got our drinks, and then she invited me to join her.

"Ah, I would love to. I wonder what happened to my friend though? Would you mind doing a quick round with me?"

"Let's do it."

It felt good being with another woman after a day with nine men. Suddenly, she felt like my Vegas partner in crime, and it had only been twenty minutes.

As we approached the edge of the dance floor, I saw Jake being escorted out by a tall security guard.

"Jake, wait up! What happened?"

Jake rubbed his head, "Sorry, Nik, I'm going back. But you

stay and have fun—"

The security guard interrupted, "Your friend here was puking in the restroom. He has to go."

"Jake…"

"Nik, you stay!"

I wasn't going to argue. I was feeling electric with a concoction of substances. I didn't want to go to the room and stare at the ceiling.

"Okay, love you, Jake."

He hugged me. "Be safe, Nik."

That night, I went out with my new friend, Tonya, and explored Las Vegas until late morning. We danced and talked about life and how she ended up in Vegas a few months prior. We wound up at a restaurant before ending the party. I loved that I was still in my clothes from the night prior. I hadn't slept, and I was intoxicated, yet I didn't feel out of place. I appreciated that about Vegas.

With the absence of the loud music of the after-hours club we left, we were able to talk more. Tonya opened up to me about her current relationship, how it was falling apart, and how she'd be forced to move out in a few weeks. She wasn't sure if she was staying in Vegas or moving back home to Florida.

"Tell me this: do you want to stay here or be home?" I asked her as we waited for our breakfast to arrive.

"I like it here. That's why I came, but I don't know if I want to do it on my own, you know? I can't stay in this relationship."

"I get it. I think you should stay then. Fuck him. You can do it without him, Tonya. Plus, you make friends so easily; look at tonight."

She smiled. "You're right. Thank you, my friend."

"Look, I know this sounds crazy, but if you decide to stay, I will move out and get a place with you." As the words left my mouth, I wondered where they came from.

She perked up. "Really? No lie? You'd move out here."

Becoming surer, I said, "Yes, 100 percent Fuck it. I'm in."

I felt the excitement of what I was committing to.

"Yes, girl, you don't even know. I need to get away from Pennsylvania! Plus, I feel like we've been friends for a lifetime." I smiled cheerfully about my new plan.

We both laughed as the waitress placed our plates of eggs and potatoes in front of us.

I lifted my bloody mary, "Cheers! A fresh start for both of us."

She grinned and clanked her glass against mine. "Fresh start, baby!"

CHAPTER 12

"We're making our final descent into Las Vegas. Flight attendants, please be seated." The pilot's announcement rattled me from my slumber. I looked out over the strip and saw the iconic black pyramid with bright, white lights shooting up through the night sky and then down toward the stratosphere tower. The twinkling lights I had just seen one month prior were now a place I called home. Reality hit me. *This is it. There is no return flight. Holy shit.*

I felt slightly panicked. For a moment, I felt overwhelmed by the shocking realization that I actually left the place I planned to escape since I was old enough to realize I could. Stuck in my head, I questioned my choices. *Why was it scary? I wanted this...Didn't I?*

Nostalgic feelings swept over me as I gathered my luggage

from baggage claim. The thought of my Grandmom, who felt like a mother to me, being so far away started to sting as I took in the surroundings of my new home. Making my way to the transportation area to wait for my ride, I pushed away heavy feelings regarding my mom and dad. We weren't speaking, which wasn't new, but moving 2,600 miles away brought up grief.

A cab pulled up and parked in front of me. I could see Tonya in the back smiling, and I felt my sadness subside.

Tonya hopped out. "Hey, girl!"

Where is her car? I didn't have my car. Rather than bug her about the car, I focused on my curiosity about our new place.

Giving her a big hug, I said, "I am so excited! I can't believe I'm really living here!"

We laughed and got my bag into the trunk of the silver sedan.

Settling in the back seat together, I had so many questions. "How is the new place?! Do we have a pool? Can't wait to see it."

"Oh, about that. It's not ready yet." Her smile faded as the sedan bounced over the speed bumps.

I felt anger. "What? Why didn't you tell me?"

"Because it's not a big deal! Don't worry; I got us a room at Mandalay Bay until it's ready."

I could see the golden lights of the Mandalay towers off in the distance; I recognized the property from my last trip.

"Okay then. Let's have a little fun until our place is ready." I smiled as I relaxed and enjoyed the short ride. I told myself this would be a mini-vacation before settling in; it would be a celebration of my new life.

Arriving at the Mandalay Bay ten minutes later, I instantly felt better. I was expecting an empty apartment, so this was an unexpected treat. A little luxury would be a nice kick-off to this transition. We rolled the luggage up the elevator to our room on the twenty-fourth floor. As we approached the room, Tonya told me her friend got us the room. When we opened the door to our suite, I smelled a familiar, unpleasant odor.

"What's the smell?" As the words rolled off my tongue, I saw an older man who appeared to be my dad's age sitting on the bed smoking a small pipe.

"What the fuck? What's going on?" My rage was back and not going anywhere. Tonya wasn't upfront about this, and I was fuming.

"Where is the money for our place?" I barked before she could answer.

"It's in the safe. Everything is just fine. Please relax, Nikki."

"How can I relax? I sold everything that I own to move here, and now I don't have a place. If you would've told me the truth, I would have waited."

"Hey now, you do have a place. You can stay here, so calm down." The man attempted to soothe me, but I was even more appalled by his steady tone, as if he were unaware that I was lied to.

My face scrunched up in anger, and I made it clear I wanted nothing to do with him. "I don't know you. Stay out of this."

I extended my shaking hand. "Tonya, give me my money. I need a drink. I am not staying here."

"Come on, Nik. Everything is in order..."

"Trust me. Don't fuck with me right now." I was so hot with anger; I felt the heat radiating off my face.

I didn't know what to do, and I couldn't think straight. I was rolling around everything I owned in two suitcases. I knew that smell; it was crystal meth. I recognized it from my aunt's place where people smoked it frequently. I didn't sign up for this shit, and I was done. I couldn't trust her. Who was I kidding? I didn't even know her.

Tonya handed me the envelope with my money. I ripped it open, surprised to find all the money there. I counted the bills, $1,400, exactly what I had sent her two weeks ago for move-in costs. At least she didn't screw me over with the money. But still, I was done with believing anything she told me.

I stuffed the envelope in my purse as Tonya attempted to talk me out of leaving.

"Just stop!" I yelled at her. "You should have told me. I would have come when the place was ready. I don't trust you, and I don't even know him. I'm out." The man sat up on the bed, looking bewildered by the chaos. I stormed out of the rancid-smelling room and didn't look back.

Within minutes, I found myself in the mirrored elevator I just rode up before I knew I was completely screwed. Staring at myself as I made my way to the ground floor, I took in my bright red cheeks as tears streamed down face. *You really fucked up this time, Nikki.*

Rolling my luggage through the casino, I scanned the expansive bright space for the nearest bar. I was still shaking and desperately needed a drink. I went straight to the first bar I saw: The Island Lounge.

With my belongings at my side, I ordered a double vodka and soda with extra lemon and sat on a comfy lounge chair next to a little table beside the bar so I could maintain some privacy.

I replayed everything that happened in my mind, punishing myself along the way. I blamed myself for rushing into this madness. Now I had nothing. I couldn't call people and tell them this happened. My family was sick of my shit; I was equally sick of theirs. I'd have to fly home and figure it out.

About thirty minutes later, the alcohol was working. My rage was reduced to anger. I looked up from my drink and saw Tonya at the bar ordering a drink. *Oh shit.* Secretly I was relieved because I felt so alone and lost. Yet I didn't want to go back with her. I couldn't trust her; she was not who I had thought she was.

She walked over with a shot of vodka for me. "I don't want you to stress. I'm so sorry. I didn't think you would be so upset. I didn't tell you because I wanted you to come. I knew we'd figure it out together."

I was able to listen to her. I saw that she was hurt by what was happening, too. It didn't matter; she was part of the reason we were homeless. I couldn't continue with our plan.

"Tonya, I feel bad that you're alone now, but so am I. I could've helped if you were honest. I can't trust you since you told me that you had the place figured out. Not to mention, I will not stay with that man. He was weird, and do you realize what he's smoking? Meth! I am not comfortable sleeping there."

I felt my mind considering forgiving her, and then I came back to my senses. *NO.* My gut told me to cut my losses.

I watched her facial expression droop in disappointment. *Not my problem,* I told myself as I took the shot.

She wasn't concerned about me when I sold all my things and flew here expecting my new home. I couldn't worry about her circumstances. I also didn't need the guilt, I had my own life to figure out. I asked her to leave, "I need space, I need to figure my life out right now. Either you leave or I will."

My body language said I was dead serious.

Watching her walk away, I wondered if I would ever see her again. I sipped my drink and decided to enjoy this moment and fly home on the first flight in morning.

It was one a.m. by then, and I thought I could catch a flight around six a.m. As I sipped on my second cocktail, I started to feel relief. Each sip seemed to amplify the Valium I had taken during my flight.

I looked over and noticed someone was paying attention to me. I felt embarrassed. I wondered how much he'd seen.

He was a tall, handsome, well-dressed man, and I noticed his watch glimmer in the light. He had big brown eyes that looked familiar in an odd way. As I watched him take a sip of his cocktail, I figured he probably made good money, and I wondered what he did for work. We were close enough to hold a conversation, but we were not close enough to reach out and shake hands.

"Is everything alright?" he asked. The tone of his voice was reassuring.

"I've had better nights." I considered if I should share it all with him. I quickly decided it didn't matter because he was a stranger I wouldn't see ever again.

"Tonight I moved here. I sold all of my things to move in with the woman who was just here." He was listening intently, nodding his head, signaling me to continue. "When I landed, there was no apartment. Instead, she brings me here to a hotel room with a strange man lounging on the bed smoking meth."

His face was still steady; he wasn't fazed by the story. "So I am going back home in the morning."

He finally smiled. "That's quite the adventure, huh? You said you sold all of your stuff. What are you going home for?"

He had witnessed the hot mess that had transpired between Tonya and me. Wasn't it obvious why I was leaving? I wasn't in the position to lie. Not in this frame of mind. In this moment, I no longer cared if I were exposing my fears and mistakes to this strange man that I happened to be attracted to. There was something about his energy that left me feeling safe with him.

I decided to be honest. I had nothing to lose; I wouldn't see this man again.

"I only moved here because I had someone to live with. The woman who was here needed a roommate, and I decided to move here with her on a whim. With all that happened tonight, this must be a sign it's not meant to be."

He didn't react immediately. First, he took it all in before carefully answering. Then he replied, "Let me see if I heard you correctly..." He was a great listener, and I wasn't used to being heard this way.

I listened intently as he recapped his understanding of what was going on. He wasn't blaming anyone or telling me I should've known better. He was coming up with solutions.

"I know you say you moved here to be her roommate, but it wasn't all about her. You wanted to be here as well, am I right?"

He made a valid point.

"Yes. But-"

"Okay, so you can't allow someone else to take you away from what you were doing for you."

Damn it. He was right. Now I felt foolish and somewhat immature.

As we sat and continued talking about the real reason I moved, over drinks, I loved how incredibly easy it was to talk to him. Dean was his name, and he had recently moved to Vegas from the Midwest. He explained he moved to check out the opportunities in Las Vegas. He said he was working with his cousin's business remotely and wanted to work in a city with more action.

I could relate to that. He seemed successful and, even more so, incredibly smart.

Three hours later, I was tired and ready to make my way to the airport. I accepted that I would be heading back to Pennsylvania with my proverbial tail tucked between my legs, declaring I fucked up and I was home. I anticipated everyone telling me, "I told you so."

Checking my phone and noticing the time, I shifted in my seat. "It's about that time. I gotta get it together and get back home."

Dean asked me a question. "What's life going to be like if you get on that plane and head home to your parent's place? You don't have a place, a car or furniture. You gotta start again."

I considered it again, this time more vividly as he guided me to remember the cold hard truth. I'd have to ask for rides, find a place to stay, and make enough money to buy a place and furnishings. I had to start again no matter where I went.

He continued with his wisdom.

"You already got this far. Do what you came to do. You don't need your friend.'

He made so much sense. His pep talk kicked my ass into gear, and he was right. I didn't need Tonya; hell, I barely knew her.

I was depending on her having a car and an apartment ready for us though. I let the reality of what he said settle in and realized I didn't want to give up on my plan. I thought about it and determined that if I went back, I could be stuck forever.

"Look, give it a month. You can rent a place where I stay. It's easy and only $800 a month for everything; plus, it's furnished," he said. He told me it was pretty much on the strip, behind the Stardust casino, so I could walk everywhere. I considered it as an alternative and weighed it against my option to fly back. I imagined going back defeated or giving this a whirl with the money I had in the envelope.

"Alright. It's an adventure, right?"

I had Dean help me carry one of my bags, and we caught a cab to his place.

It was about four thirty a.m., and the sky was still dark but brightening. We pulled up to his place.

It was dumpy. It reminded me of an older hotel at the Jersey Shore that was on its way out. Laughing at myself in disbelief that I was in this situation, I stepped out of the cab and straightened my black sundress that I had been wearing for nearly twenty-four hours now. We walked up to the main office and noticed it was closed. I read the sign that said it opened at seven a.m.

Damn it. Feeling exhausted, I looked at Dean for another solution.

"Look, I know you just met me, but if you feel comfortable staying at my place until it opens, you're welcome to. We can get you settled when the office opens."

Twenty minutes later, I was in my pajamas about to climb into the bed of a man I had just met hours ago. I was attracted to him, but I didn't want him to get the wrong idea. Sex was the last thing on my mind with all that happened. I hoped he felt the same. As I listened to him brushing his teeth, I got nervous, I hoped I was right about him and that he didn't murder me in my sleep or, worse, while I was awake.

He handed me a bottle of water and said, "I set my alarm for nine a.m., so we can get breakfast and get your room." I was surprised he had a plan for me; this was comforting.

"Thank you. I appreciate your help." Settling in, I felt safe again.

"Good night," he said softly as he rolled over and away from me to sleep.

CHAPTER 13

My first month in Vegas felt like an extended vacation that I didn't want to end. I suppose in some ways I didn't think it would; I thought it could only get better. I spent most of my days and all of my nights with Dean.

We would walk next door to the Stardust for breakfast most mornings. We'd keep ourselves busy on our own for the afternoon, and at night, we'd head to dinner and out for the night. He and I were both new to the city, so we explored and enjoyed all of it together.

We walked through the forum shops, arms locked and pleasantly drunk from our drinks at lunch. I couldn't do this on my own; I would have run out of money within days living this way. Dean paid for everything, which felt nice as it took the stress off my job hunt which was moving super slowly and without much success.

I found it strange that Dean didn't speak about his work, nor did I see him do much, yet I was not going to question it; this was a special kind of paradise for me.

There were some downsides to living where we lived. The precise location was not ideal, although it was very convenient because I was without a car. I could walk to most places; the strip was my backyard, but I didn't feel safe walking except during the day. Within in my first few days, I was approached by two men in our parking lot who thought I was a prostitute.

I saw them later that night with Dean, and he clarified that they were pimps living here in search of women to work for them. This blew my mind. The women were selling their bodies and then they'd happily give up their profits?

Apparently, the men made the women feel safe out in the streets. Our place was prime location for dancers, pimps, and prostitutes because it was directly across the street from two strip clubs on Industrial Blvd.

This side of the city was sketchy yet fascinating. I worked at my small club in Philly, which seemed like child's play compared to what I witnessed within weeks here.

Dean and I would talk about where we wanted to move next. Everything felt so right that I began to feel grateful for what happened with Tonya, and I forgave her. If she had not lied, I wouldn't have met Dean, and suddenly, I couldn't imagine life any other way.

Just weeks into our inseparable friendship, our chemistry took over, and I gave into the sexual tension.

It felt risky because our friendship was a refuge for me; I had become codependent, which wasn't new; living here without him wouldn't be the same. I was afraid to lose myself, but it was too late. I was now afraid to lose him.

This definitely wasn't what I had imagined for my next relationship; I hoped to remain single to work on myself for a bit, find a job at a casino, and enjoy life as a twenty-two-year-old.

Prior to my move to Vegas, I found myself in a brief relationship with a man who became incredibly jealous and lost it one night, choking me and punching me in the face. After breaking things off with him, he came by my place late at night. I heard him outside; he was calling my phone, but I wasn't playing games this time around. I called 9-1-1, and he was arrested for trespassing. That's when I recognized the destructive pattern with men that hurt me. Why was I attracted to them? How did they find me? My friends weren't struggling with this. That last attempt at dating was all I needed to know that I was in need of a fresh start. Thankfully, Dean was different. I could tell; he wasn't desperate or insecure. His confidence was magnetic. I was totally pulled in.

His magnetism wasn't felt by me alone. He had a handful of female friends who he made before we met. His phone would light up late at night, and I caught a glimpse of the names. All women. I hadn't met them; we went out to the lounges and clubs often, but we were always alone. He told me about the women, but it didn't bother me initially. At least, that's what I told myself. Plus, we were always together, so I didn't feel threatened by any of it. We spent hours lying in Dean's bed together, watching movies on a tiny laptop and laughing at ourselves for enjoying it. We were falling in love; we both knew it. My room was there, but I used it for changing my clothes and showering. After I was fresh, I would return to his place, and all was well, comfortable even. One day his behavior shifted, and that's when we began to change.

It was late afternoon when I returned to his place. I was in a black cotton romper and flip-flops. My hair was still wet. The desert heat was suffocating as I stood in front of Dean's door, waiting for him to let me in. "Where the fuck is he?" I asked under my breath as I reached to knock for the fourth time.

The neighbor opened the door with his shirt off, smoking a cigarette as if he just woke up.

"Damn, Shorty, you still think he's in there?"

Stunned by his straightforwardness, I just looked at him for a moment.

"He could be asleep," I said. I felt stupid and slightly panicked.

"Nah, I was asleep, and you woke me up knocking like the goddamn police."

I gave him a look that said, "Fuck you." I turned to walk home.

My room was eight doors down from Dean's, on the corner of the building, but I pretty much lived with him. He didn't tell me he was going anywhere, so where could he be?

For the next four hours, I fumbled around my apartment, attempting to tame my anxiety. Was he with another woman? My mind created narratives to freak me out and spin me into paranoia. I walked across the street to the mini-mart to purchase beer to take the edge off. I felt how unhealthy this was. He wasn't my man;

I couldn't be upset. I had no right, right? Tell that to my insides that were squirming with the potential of betrayal from my new best friend with benefits. I couldn't handle the self-hatred in my head. Within fifteen minutes, I was back in my place, attempting to drown out the noise in my head.

As I sat on my bed, taking big gulps of my beer to calm down, there was a knock on my door. I took one more sip of the bitter-tasting beer to deal with whatever bullshit he was going to tell me.

I swung open the door and looked at him, waiting for his apologies, but nothing came.

"Umm, where were you?" Hearing myself, I realized I sounded slightly crazy. I reminded myself to keep it cool; I wanted to keep him around.

"I was making money." He spoke without hesitation, moving past me to have a seat on the bed.

I shut the door, wanting to scream at him for his relaxed responses.

"Really. What does that even mean?"

He smirked; he found my frustration amusing. This pissed me off even more. He was up to something, or he was seeing another woman.

"Not funny. So tell me how you're making money."

He laughed at me.

"No, really. I'm curious." I hoped I hadn't crossed any boundaries by asking about his business.

"I've been hustlin'. Mostly to taxi drivers. I do it here and there. I need a better connect though; that's what I was handling today."

I was relieved to know it wasn't another woman. I felt my tension melt away.

"Oh, okay. I see. You didn't have to hide that from me. I was worried about you!" As I said that I felt like such a fraud. I wasn't worried about him; I was worried about him leaving me.

I watched him open the fridge for a can of beer, wondering if I should share my past or leave it behind me.

"I actually sold powder before moving out here." I watched his face for a response before continuing.

"If you want a better connection, you should let me ask Tonya. She knows a bunch of people, but you know her crew..."

We both laughed, thinking of the night we met.

"Alright. You can do that later. Let's go eat."

We picked back up as if nothing had happened. I felt crazy for the paranoid mess that I was.

The next day, I reached out to Tonya because I wanted to help Dean. I wanted to get this for him because I wanted to be irreplaceable to him, so I shifted into pleasing mode. Once I was comfortable with a man, I got scared; I wanted to keep him so I overcompensated.

Fortunately, Tonya knew someone. She wanted to please me, so she hooked us up. Within hours of my call to Tonya, Dean was in the parking lot waiting on Vic, Tonya's connect.

Dean was in the parking lot for nearly an hour, which made me nervous. It meant one of two things: it was going well and the two men hit it off, or something was wrong. Eventually Dean came upstairs, and immediately I could tell he was pleased with whatever happened. He opened the paper bag in his hand and dumped out the biggest bag of cocaine I had ever seen.

"Now *this* is something I can work with." He grinned as he set up the scale on the small battered, wooden table.

Men like Dean sold drugs, but they don't use them. They looked down on the people who used. I couldn't show him that part of me. Plus, I basically quit since I was in Vegas with no access. I drank and slept. I didn't mind because I had him. My needs were met.

I felt differently with the mound of cocaine sitting in front of my face. I was overcome by an intense craving.

I loved watching his excitement, as if he just came home with a new toy. Then he let me in on the low pricing and how much money he could make with what he bought. I understood the excitement. Then he told me his plan to double the cocaine he bought through "stretching it." I had never done this myself, but I heard of people doing it. He explained that he would compound vitamins to nearly double the weight to make more money. I was skeptical and slightly disgusted when I thought of all the bullshit I must've snorted in my days. Not that cocaine was healthy even in its purest form.

We left the apartment in a cab to get supplies at the store. He purchased a large bottle of the powdery vitamin supplement. Next, we hit up Wal-Mart for a Pyrex, rectangular, glass baking dish and a bottle of acetone. This blew my mind in the worst way. I asked him twice, "Acetone? As in nail polish remover?" He responded both times with, "yes."

Back at his place, Dean broke out the supplies and turned the small wooden table into a makeshift drug laboratory. He pulled the ounces out of the cabinet and then took out a small box that held a scale. This cocaine was a flaky texture with the glisten of mother of pearl. It was the most beautiful batch I'd seen, and I couldn't believe he was going to ruin it with this crap.

I watched curiously as he poured a few ounces into the Pyrex and mashed it all down into a powder. Next, he added an equal amount of the vitamin into the mixture. He poured just enough acetone to moisten the mixture. After it was mixed up, he pressed into the bottom of the glass dish until the powder compounded into a small white brick, which he microwaved for fifteen-second intervals until the process was complete.

Dean let it cool and then loosened the newly formed slab of cocaine from the Pyrex. He broke it down into smaller pieces and began weighing and bagging.

He had effectively doubled his initial purchase. Just like that, money. It was magical to create so much money like this.

Dean began moving product quickly. He built relationships with a few dancers across the street, which I didn't like, but I told myself that this was funding our fun and hopefully our new place in the future. The dancers loved it when their clients bought this stuff. It meant they would be up later to spend more money on them. These women were all hustlers, so of course they bought a bag for $60 and charged the client $120. Everything went for a premium. Welcome to Las Vegas, the land of upcharges and sheisty deals.

After watching what Dean moved, I began running numbers in my mind. Excitement moved through me as I realized the gold mine I had access to. I thought back to Warren and his "logistics" business. He would fly with the product a lot of the times. If he could move this operation through the air to Pennsylvania, I could too. I could sell weight there. Rather than small grams I used to deal with, I would sell ounces. I knew this money would change our lives quickly. This was a way out of the life I knew.

Plus, I liked to gamble, and though this was an all-in kind of bet, I saw no other way of making large amounts of money this quickly. THIS was my way out. I was desperate for change. I wanted to do this, so I told him my idea.

When I first shared the idea to hustle back home, Dean looked at me like I was nuts. He couldn't understand how this would work, but I shared some ideas. I had flown with weed and ecstasy to Jamaica for personal use when I was eighteen. I told him that I knew friends who did the same. I knew it would work.

He laughed at my audacity. To prove my point, I reached out to some potential customers and gauged the interest. Like I thought, they wanted it. The people I knew were buying junk for $1,000-$1,200 an ounce. You would think ours was crap after what Dean did to cut it, but it was still better than what they were used to buying back home.

I had a plan to fly across the country with cocaine strapped to my body for the sake of making more money than I had ever held in my hands before. This twisted plan existed more than anything else in my life; it represented freedom to me. I knew I could live an entirely different lifestyle, and I was desperate for it. Not only did the idea of the new life drive me, I knew I would make Dean happy. At this rate, I would be irreplaceable. I bet the other women he had calling his phone wouldn't do this. This realization soothed my insecurities.

After a bit of convincing, Dean agreed to purchase my roundtrip flight to Philadelphia. I had three days to prepare myself.

CHAPTER 14

The day came, and I was regretting what I had planned to do, but I didn't mention it to Dean. He spent the day carefully preparing the product. Everything was weighed out perfectly and sealed tightly with a vacuum contraption that sucked all the air from the package. I was flying home with a quarter of a kilogram— nine ounces of cocaine. We poured the iridescent white powder into their bags, flattened the bags out, and stored them all in one quart Ziploc bag. This bag was placed in the front of my pelvis. For added support, I wore Spandex high-waisted shorts to suck everything in as tightly as possible. I wore my favorite comfortable sweatpants and loose T-shirt that didn't show my waistline; I layered everything with a hoodie.

I took a Xanax and drank vodka with a splash of Sprite at

Dean's place before leaving. I sipped my drink, but I could tell he was nervous for me as I watched him pace the small room. The mood was solemn as I waited for the cab to arrive. We were both quiet, and although I didn't say it, I believed we were both thinking the same thing: *I may not return from this.* As I hugged Dean, it crossed my mind that this could be the last time I saw him. I wondered if he'd be supportive if I were arrested. I pushed the possibility out of my mind and focused on the goal.

In the cab to the airport, I realized I was buzzed but not as numb as I would like to be. Dean warned me about getting too drunk; he was right. I needed to be aware enough to pull this off. While he was right, I was the one committing a federal crime that could lock me away for decades. I would decide how numb I wanted to be.

During my short cab ride, I shifted my focus to my goal. I was going to make $12,000 in three days. That was one-third of my annual salary just one year prior. I held my vision for a profitable run and promised myself I'd take another shot of vodka before the security line.

Climbing out of the cab, I could feel the plastic Ziploc digging into my waist. I ignored it, grabbing my carry-on bag and making my way through the crowded sidewalk and into the McCarran Airport. Waiting in line, I could feel the intense energy of the ticketing counters and all the travelers waiting in line. After twenty minutes in line, I was checked into my flight. As the ticketing agent printed my boarding pass, I looked to the left and noticed the police at the end of the ticket counter. I had to remind myself to calm down as my paranoia kicked in. *They aren't here for you. You're golden. No one knows anything. It's all in your head.*

The voice in my head was guiding and comforting me. I had one goal: that was to get through security. As I made my way up the escalator silently, my inner-dialogue was anything but quiet. *Why would I get caught? I don't have a gun and no metal. No one is going to touch me. Therefore, I am safe. Keep going.*

After a quick pit stop in the bathroom to readjust myself for the security line, I walked out and headed to the escalator that led to TSA line. Just as I was about to step into line with my carry-on bag and purse, I decided to turn left to take a quick shot at TGI Fridays. If I were going to jail, at least I wouldn't be sober.

As I sat on the wooden barstool, awaiting my double shot of vodka, I took in the scenery. I saw the faces of travelers and wondered where they were going and who they were leaving behind. I considered that this could be my last moment of freedom. I told myself to enjoy it, and then I dismissed the option that I would be anything but successful in my plan. I threw back the cold, clear alcohol and felt the liquid relief move through my body. I knew it was time.

The security line was moving swiftly. My redeye was leaving at 11:45 p.m., and I had plenty of time. An older, unsuspecting woman checked my ID and boarding pass and waved me through. *Almost there.* There were maybe twenty people ahead of me before my turn to walk through the metal detector. My heart was pounding, and my nerves cut through the alcohol as I stepped closer to the search area. I placed my purse in the bin. As I bent down to pick up my shoes, I could feel the bags crumple against my waist. I turned to walk through the metal detector. I was behind one man and then it was me. *Oh shit. It's time.* I watched the man walk through the gray archway without a beep.

My turn. I stepped forward with confidence, knowing that my body language mattered. *You're safe. You got this.* I smiled at the security officer waiting on the other side for me. I was smiling partly because I wanted to be nice, but also, I realized I was making it through; my plan worked. I stepped forward and made my way through to claim my belongings.

Walking away from the security area, I wanted to jump and celebrate. I was clear. *Holy shit, I did it!* I had another drink at the next bar I found and took my seat. The adrenaline rush of what I had just done woke me up. I was sober. I texted Dean to let him know I was having a drink to signal I was okay. He was proud of me, and this felt better than any amount of money. I craved his validation just as I longed for my father's. Getting a man to truly notice me was like medicine for me.

It felt good to make it through the line and onto my plane, yet the paranoia didn't end there. As we landed in Philadelphia nearly six hours later, I imagined FBI agents waiting for me at the gate. Perhaps they wanted me to transport it to get me with more charges. I didn't feel safe until I was in my girlfriend's car as we drove away from the airport. Right then, I knew I had made it.

In Pennsylvania, everything went exactly as planned. My family wondered why I was back so soon. I told them I had to handle some things. They suspected something, I could tell, but it didn't matter. They knew the life I lived; I learned it from them.

Within forty-eight hours, I quickly sold everything, but I stashed two grams of the uncut stuff for myself, which I did with my friend Monica as she and I ran around together for two days, making my runs. We had fun that weekend, and when it was time to go, I prepared the money to fly back. Large amounts of money are suspicious at the airport, as is depositing an amount over $9,999 at a bank. From what Dean warned me, this was a red-flag for suspicious behavior. As directed, I wrapped the money in a Ziploc and placed it in my pants just like the powder and made my way back to Las Vegas.

Dean was so proud of me when I returned. He was even impressed. That made me feel good, better than the money. I craved his affection more than dollars. It's what I wanted my entire life, and I never realized I would find the nourishment I desired this way. Earning that much money gave me a sense of pride. I knew Dean wouldn't leave me now, and this twisted truth comforted me.

CHAPTER 15

Our business partnership cemented our intimate relationship. Dean and I acknowledged we were together, and I turned in my key to the room I barely inhabited. At first, this felt dreamy; we were like best friends who also had great sex and took massive risks together. I felt like I had nothing else to live for, so to me, it was worth the risk.

My official move into Dean's place didn't change much except that now my luggage was on his bedroom floor. However, knowing that I was there and couldn't leave affected our dynamic. He began to have moods where he wouldn't speak to me for hours; he would respond with one-word responses or completely shut down. As if this weren't bad enough, I'd see his phone blowing up with calls from women all the time. I told myself it was just money and nothing else, yet my heart told me differently. There was one woman who called the most, and he would jump for her. We were on the second floor where I could peek out the blinds and see whom he was meeting. One afternoon, after watching him sulk around and ignore me, I heard his phone ring, and he responded with a much more joyful tone than I had heard all day. "Cool, I'll be right out." He then walked out of the door, and I snuck over to the window to take a look.

It was the same white SUV I saw pick him up last week. It felt like a punch to the gut as I watched the pretty, tanned blond jump out and give him a big hug. *He didn't hug me like that for days*, I thought. My jealousy forced me away from the window; I couldn't deal with what I saw.

I was irritated, but when he got upstairs, I said nothing. I kept to myself. Later, during a movie, I was so distracted by my new obsession: the blonde. My insecure curiosity felt like it was eating away at my stomach; I was anxious and had trouble sitting still. I had to ask him about her.

"What's up with your friend? Were you guys hooking up before I came along?"

He looked at me funny, as if he were confused. "No. We're just cool. She's my customer; that's it."

"Okay...." I said in my if-that's-what-you-want-to-say tone.

I stuffed my fears down inside and ignored what I felt. I told myself that I was lucky and that I was the one here with him. *Fuck her*, I thought.

At this point, I barely spoke to anyone back home until it was time to go back for a run to make money. Even then, I felt paranoid to leave Dean, as his behavior led me to not trust him.

There were more women customers than I could count, but he assured me that's all they were. My need for love rationalized his odd behavior.

Dean and I had our first fight when he went out to make a *quick* delivery to the white SUV and didn't come home for six hours, ignoring my calls.

He seemed amused that I cared about his whereabouts. He told me to chill out and explained that this was what needed to happen for us to stick to our financial plan and move out. The money I made back East was added to the money he was making, and he invested all of it into more product. We decided I would fly back East and make money a few more times to create a cushion, and then I'd stop. The end goal was to give us both a life better than we knew and then go legal. What I didn't realize at the time was that's what everyone in the drug game says. But the fast money is addictive, perhaps more addictive than the product for some.

Over the next few weeks, our lives became more intertwined. Dean asked me to get everything in my name. He explained that his credit was horrible, and it would be easier if I applied for everything. While this may make the average twenty-two-year-old suspicious, it made me feel secure. Everything was in my name; therefore, it was more mine than his. Beyond that, I took it as a commitment from him, which was delusional. It felt like insurance on our relationship. A car, cell phones, and soon our new townhouse were all placed in my name.

As time passed, our fun times dwindled. We spent fewer nights out together; I was home waiting for him to return from his runs around the city to "work." It began to feel like I was spending my life waiting for him. Dean knew how to pull me in deeper when I was at the end of my rope. After days of frustration, he'd return with shopping bags filled with beautiful clothing and Gucci bags, which were my favorite. No matter how suspicious I was, his thoughtfulness conflicted with my fears. I never had anyone shop for me. My ex-boyfriends took from me. I was used to neglect and abandonment, but these gifts made things feel different. This had to be real love, right? I decided yes. *This is real love*, I thought. *He gives to me. He's thoughtful.* This was new, and I wasn't willing to give this up. *I'm his.*

I continued to battle myself silently until he could no longer hide his behavior. One morning, my worries were magnified when Dean got a call. He and I were lying in bed while I was awake and he was still asleep from his night out. His phone started ringing, but with the ringtone version of Mariah Carey's "We Belong Together," My heart dropped. I thought: *How in the fuck will you talk your way out of this one?* The ring tone ended, and then it went off again. *Oh, and they are blowing you up on top of that?*

He jumped out of bed and took the phone into the bathroom.

Is this motherfucker serious right now? I couldn't hear what he was saying since it was super muffled, but I was replaying what I would say after. *The fucking nerve of this guy. I've been staying with him for nearly three months, and now there's THAT song as his ringtone?*

I couldn't sit still while he was in the bathroom. I paced in a circle on my side of the bedroom. I was livid, so much so that I was nauseous. I felt like every cell in my body was screaming at me to get out of the relationship right now. Yet, as angry as I was, I was far from prepared to walk away from him.

Twenty minutes later, he emerged from the bathroom, and he looked frustrated. He went outside to smoke a cigarette and came in, knowing he was in for it.

"What was that about, and who was that?" I was in full-on bitch mode. I was feeling so disrespected.

He replied with a tone that declared he was not going there. "It nothing. It's an ex, and that was her favorite song. Old ringtone. We're not talking about this."

His tone was startling. It was familiar. He sounded like the men I dated who hurt me. Except he was different—I knew he wouldn't hurt me—we were different. I knew I pushed some of the men before, so I listened to what I felt and decided to be cool this time around. I felt a good woman was one who listened, was loyal, and allowed men space to be who they are. I reminded myself to be a *good* woman, although rage was welling up inside.

We sat for some time in silence, yet my anger felt loud. I couldn't be still. I wanted clarity, and I wanted to know everything. *Make it better, motherfucker.* Then he got dressed and went out for runs without anything but a casual, "I'll be back later." I felt left alone with unanswered questions. My heart was aching in the townhouse that started feeling like a lonely prison.

Las Vegas was a twenty-four-hour town and a drug dealer's

paradise. When we woke up at nine a.m., there were people just ending their midnight shifts in the casino and heading to a local bar that was also twenty-four hours. When he was out drinking at a bar with his customers, where was I? At home, waiting for a word from him. But that night, after the ringtone fiasco, I had enough of being the doormat. *Fuck that.* I decided I was going to enjoy myself, too.

I got dressed up like I did when I first arrived. I took a bit of the powder out of the kitchen cabinet and did some. I called Tonya, and we went out. After all the stress of our moving mishap, we had worked on our friendship. We both needed one another's support. Plus, I knew no one else in the area, which was also one of the reasons I felt so isolated. My being alone without friendship added to my insecurities. I sat alone in my worries nearly nonstop. Tonya and I went out for drinks at a lounge and ended up at the club.

That night, I avoided my phone on purpose. I wanted to be more like Dean. The club was emptying out, and I was tipsy. I knew it was late so I turned on my phone to check the time. I had eight text messages from Dean. He was probably worried. *Good,* I thought. *Now he knows how I feel.* I texted him that I was coming home, feeding him a dose of his own medicine.

He responded almost instantly. "DON'T."

What the fuck?

"Of course I'm coming there. That's my home. What's your problem?"

Then nothing. My place was fifteen minutes from the Bellagio; I got there quickly without telling Tonya what was happening.

The taxi dropped me off at home. I unlocked the door to find Dean sitting stiffly on the sofa, eyes glued to the TV, yet his demeanor was malicious.

"Your clothes are in the dumpster."

I thought he was kidding. I looked in my closet, and my stuff was gone. "What the fuck?" I walked out back to the dumpster where I saw my blue luggage sitting on top.

"What the hell, Dean? How could you? Go get my fucking suitcase."

"It's not my shit. I'm not getting anything."

Who was this man? I didn't recognize him. The man I loved didn't treat me this way. I was dramatic, drunk, and crying hysterically now. I was hurt, and I knew this feeling: the sting of betrayal by a loved one.

"You did this, Dean. Make it right! Go get it."

He didn't budge off the sofa. He wouldn't look at me as he blamed me.

"You did this to yourself. Think you can leave and ignore me? Okay. Go get your things before the trash truck comes."

How could he do this to me? He was supposed to be different.

I folded over and cried on the living room floor. The pain stunned me. I felt like I was now living with my enemy. How did I not see this coming?

"Please go get my stuff. Make it right!" My sobs were my last hope for him making this better, as if he could magically erase what happened. The damage was done, but my mind worked to protect my illusion. His refusal to help led me to question who was actually guilty here. *Did I fuck up?*

He wouldn't look at me; he was absolutely certain I was wrong. His certainty led me to scan my night and my behavior. I must have done something wrong.

I couldn't believe he turned on me. I wanted to fix this rift between us and have our life back. I wanted to stay with Dean and work it out. I sat next to him on the sofa, sobbing. I went into relationship-saving mode because I felt I couldn't lose him. Not at that moment. I suddenly regretted my choices.

"We have a plan. I'm not leaving." I glared at him, waiting for his response. He wouldn't look at me.

"I went out because I was hurt by you leaving me constantly. Let's fix this, please Dean. Pleeease,"

Hurt by his behavior, I still felt more afraid to leave him. He'd been the best thing to happen to me my entire life. This is what I believed as I clung to the memories of our first month together. I couldn't go; I wouldn't go.

I pleaded with him. I was by his side for another twenty minutes before he turned my way and began to soften. After promising that I would never behave this way again, I asked him to help me lift my things out of the dumpster.

"Come on, please. I am too short. I can't reach in there and lift it all out."

This time he agreed. I felt like I won. He managed to successfully manipulate me into believing I did something wrong. The relationship went downhill and fast.

I was too weak to leave, so I hoped that was the last of our tumultuous times. We were both drunk that night; he was out doing his thing and so was I. *Shit happens*, I thought. I lay down to sleep and replayed the beautiful times from just two months ago when I found my best friend, the man who I just *knew* would never hurt me. In fact, he kind of saved me.

As we continued to settle into our new place, I noticed my period was a week late. I thought it was no big deal since I figured it must be from the stress of the move. I was pregnant before and remembered feeling sick, so I felt safe knowing I didn't feel that same way.

Another week passed and still no period. My boobs were sensitive and heavy. I went to Walgreens, and I bought a test, deciding that I would go home and get it out of the way.

I didn't feel pregnant, not like the last time. My period had been late before. I was drinking and getting high more and more. To get out of the house more, I had started hustling in the casino lounges. Dean didn't see a reason for me to go out for fun. If I were going out, I needed to make money. So, I did what I had to do. I also numbed myself along the way. I would sneak off into the restroom to do a line and then sit with a cocktail and talk to men who looked like they were up for a good time. This was my typical night. Oftentimes, I would join the men at the club and hang at their table with them. It was my escape for the night. But suddenly I was feeling sick, and I didn't want to go out. That's when I knew something was off.

I peed on the stick and waited.

One line appeared on the stick and then another. Frantically,

I checked the instructions on the box. Checked the stick. Checked the box. I flashbacked to the day it must've happened. We had an accident, but I brushed it off optimistically due to my cycle timing.

I stared in the bathroom mirror with tears welling up in my eyes. *I can't do this*, I thought. I wasn't ready for this and not with him.

Fuck.

Dean had become progressively more controlling, and I didn't want this life. Maybe later, but first we needed to fix us. I wondered if it was too late to get along better. I needed to know that before making lifelong commitments, such as raising a child together. I was shaking. The nausea came as I prepared to tell Dean what was happening. It hit me that I shouldn't stay with a man I wasn't willing to have a child with. In that moment, I saw that I was staying because he had become my addiction, but I knew a child didn't need this dynamic. I took a long look at myself, stopping at my pelvis, and I realized that once again I was not alone. I tossed my hair into a ponytail, turned on the faucet, and splashed cold water on my face until I felt ready to face Dean.

Eventually, I made it downstairs to find Dean eating a bowl of cereal, completely consumed by a football game. I stood there for a moment, waiting for him to look away from the TV and notice me. Finally, a commercial came on, and he saw me standing at the edge of the living room.

He knew something was off, "What's wrong?"

"I'm pregnant."

The words being spoken out loud spun me into an ugly cry.

Dean looked up and smiled. "Why are you crying?" He got up

to comfort me. I stood there, feeling trapped by this pregnancy. More specifically, I felt trapped in this relationship. "I'm crying because our lifestyle and our relationship isn't ready for a baby."

"It's okay," he said as he hugged me. "We can handle it."

Inside, I felt heavy and depressed by this. I would be home pregnant and alone while Dean ran the city all night long. I was only twenty-two, and I wasn't ready for this. He had no idea that I was getting high so often. I felt like I needed to drink; it wasn't a choice. It was medicine at this point.

"I'm sure we could, but I'm not sure I want to. I don't feel ready, Dean."

Looking at him for sympathy, he pulled me down playfully to sit on the sofa with him. Taken aback by his joy, I was confused. I didn't feel celebratory. I didn't want to sit still, nor did I want to play. I wanted to worry, it would drive me to find a solution that felt good. I was anxious at the thought of bringing a child into the life we were living. "No, I don't know if I can do this. Actually, I can't."

"Look, you aren't having an abortion, so you can get that thought out of your head. You can do this. You're going to do it."

He looked at me, waiting for me to agree. Suddenly, I felt like a prisoner. His temper was getting worse; I didn't want to say no in this moment. I would have to figure it out on my own.

Swallowing down my disagreement, I took a deep breath and nuzzled my head into his shoulder to end the conversation.

I didn't see myself as a mother. I couldn't imagine it. I couldn't even hold a job, and I was abusing my body daily to deal with myself. I was the epitome of irresponsible.

I didn't say anything else to him. I looked up Planned Parenthood and made an appointment for the following week. I needed to get clarity around this. I wasn't ready. I had to figure this out for myself. He couldn't control my body. I was scared by this relationship and this pregnancy.

Dean and I had conversations about children, and he knew I didn't plan to be a mother. On the other hand, he was excited. He said the baby would bring a lot to both of us.

Two days before my secret clinic appointment arrived, I woke up to what appeared to be my period; I was bleeding. It looked like my period, and while I didn't want to be pregnant, I found this upsetting. Was I able to have children?

To be safe, Dean drove me to Spring Valley Hospital to get checked out. We waited for an hour and a half to be seen for a simple pregnancy blood test that quickly confirmed that I was not pregnant. The doctor had deemed that the bleeding was a miscarriage. I was relieved that I had a chance to get my messy life together on my own.

CHAPTER 16

After the miscarriage, I went on about my life as usual, which was anything but ordinary to the average person. The holidays came and went, bringing with them the familiar feelings of loneliness. During the holidays, I craved a sense of warmth and family togetherness that I had never experienced. Yet the yearning was real. As I watched people getting together, I wondered what it was like to be a part of a family that loved each other. In our home, my mom would drink too much and make comments to my dad until he would get angry enough to flip out. She wanted attention, and when she got it, then all hell would break loose.

Hate was more prevalent than happiness during the holidays in our home. While I knew my family usually disappointed my holiday expectations, I missed them, nevertheless, during my first season living that far away. I opted to spend Christmas with Dean, and we ate at a local restaurant. I was in the bathroom doing what I did, sneaking bumps of cocaine. I was becoming depressed by the isolation I was feeling in Vegas.

Bi-weekly trips to Pennsylvania boosted our savings and kept me entertained, but in-between, I felt alone. The depression and loneliness I would feel in Pennsylvania had found its way back to me nearly 3,000 miles away. I began to realize that I couldn't lose the darkness, I carried it with me. Dean and I were quieter than we were when we met. I felt I couldn't share everything with him. He began to feel more like an authority figure than a lover.

He was a mentor to me. I loved him, and I was attracted to him, but I didn't feel safe like I once did with him. I kept myself busy until my next run to Pennsylvania.

While I was in Pennsylvania, I always felt good when I sold everything I brought and deposited the money in the bank in several drops. I knew the person working the counter would wonder where I got the money, but I didn't care. Maybe they assumed I was dancing, that my boyfriend gave me money, or a man gave it to me for sex. I didn't really care. I was making money, and that was my goal. I believed fulfillment would come with more money and that all the metaphoric dirt on me would be washed clean. I would be worthy, finally, of the sort of love and affection I needed. Beyond the need for external validation, I believed I would have the courage to leave if I had more of a cushion. This mindset became an illness and sickness of the heart and mind. I believed money could cure all.

Within a few months, my entire family knew what I was doing on my travels, and they weren't shocked by it. Did they like it? No. However, it made no real difference whether they liked it or not; they saw how much money I made. If it made money, it made sense to them.

While I was away, Dean would go silent. I would call and get no response for the day, and sometimes I wouldn't hear from him until the following morning. I was insecure and emotionally unstable. I would think, *I hate him and I'm done.* Then I would think, *I love him. I can't lose him. This will work out.* My mind painted vivid images of him sleeping with other women to him falling asleep alone in front of the TV.

To soothe my fears of him with other women, I reminded myself of how we were meant to be. I would remember the synchronistic way we met and immediately felt an unwillingness to let him go. *Hold on, Nikki. You can't leave yet.* This was before I understood that people come into our lives for a season or reason, not necessarily meant to stay. I wanted everyone I cared for to be lifetime material. The night in Pennsylvania when I didn't hear back from Dean, I couldn't sleep. I stayed up all night partying with friends. When the bars closed, I checked my phone only to realize there was nothing from him. Then I would snap. Abandonment took over, and I turned into an anxious mess. I left voicemails and text messages threatening him that I would not come home again and that I would keep the money to have a fresh start in Philly. Soon he would reach out, and I would then ignore his calls or extend my stay to avoid him. I played this game to shift the power until he begged me to return. Once he begged me to come back, I felt good again. I felt wanted and needed, and when I did, I went back.

This quickly became a pattern for us, and I was aware that my parents did this, too. My dad wouldn't come home for days while he was doing his thing until my mom would snap, threatening to leave. At times, she did leave, picking up with us three young kids and moving away, but then she came back. These were patterns of pain.

When I returned to Vegas, Dean picked me up in the car, and I could see the sparkle of glitter all over the black leather interior. My heart sank; I *knew* it.

"I know you've been with someone. Who the fuck is she?" Dean didn't say a word. He just drove and turned up the music on me. I was now yelling at him. "Answer me! I want to know the truth!"

He backhanded me, and I fell back in my seat.

I was shocked.

He's mad? He's the one not responding to me. When I travel, he's cheating! The glitter spoke for him. I hated him for hitting me and for having someone else in my car for so long that my car was covered with *her.*

"Shut the fuck up. I had a customer in the car. I'm tired of listening to you!" He was done with the conversation, and I knew better than to say any more.

Bullshit. I knew he was lying; I just knew it.

As we drove home, I felt the same disgust I once felt for my ex.

How did we get here? How did my best friend turn into this heartless asshole driving me home? Why did I pick these men? I was so sick of myself for falling into these situations. When we got home, I immediately wanted to leave again. I wished I were back in Pennsylvania. He went up to the bedroom and turned the music up obnoxiously loud, and I heard the shower turn on. He was going out.

I thought about taking my suitcase and escaping back to Pennsylvania while he showering, but I was too exhausted. The life felt like it had been squeezed out of me. I was tender. I didn't have it in me to leave. I sat on the sofa and cried alone, wondering if this would get better or worse. I was so drained that I fell asleep and didn't even hear him go out.

Most nights, when he went for his runs, he didn't return until the morning. It *was* a city that never slept, and I could see he *was* making money, so I bit my tongue more because I wasn't ready to move back to Pennsylvania. I wasn't ready to give up yet. Sometimes I saw him come home with glitter on his clothing or with another woman's foundation on his shirt. It was out of hand. I made up stories to validate his lies and make myself feel better: *I hug men; my makeup could end up on them, too.*

I found evidence for whatever I was looking for, and I wasn't ready for the truth. Not yet.

Two weeks later, I found myself ill on my bi-weekly money run. I didn't feel well enough to drink on the plane, which was a bizarre circumstance since I normally always had something to ease my nerves. I felt like I was wasting the trip in first class without drinking, which was the best part, in my opinion. The idea of sipping a cocktail made me gag; that's when I knew I was not well. Upon my arrival, I felt off, increasingly more nauseous and foggy. After completing my various stops, I headed to my mom's to lay on her sofa. This also signaled that I was sick; I wouldn't lie on my mom's sofa in the middle of the day if I were well. I would be out day drinking with friends until my flight the next day.

I asked her to make me soup, and she did, but I started to feel worse. My abdomen felt tight. I was bloated, and I began worrying that something had gone wrong with my miscarriage a few months ago. My mom took me into the Chester County Hospital, which was the same hospital I was born in. It wasn't long before I was checked in and waiting to be seen, and I had an uneasy feeling. I knew something was off, and my hypochondria was activated.

While back in triage, they gave me a quick check, and I told them about my high stress-levels and the fact that that I had a miscarriage three months prior. My vitals were normal, but the nurse advised that I go back for an ultrasound.

Fifteen minutes later, I was lying down on a cold, paper sheet that lined the bed with my feet in stirrups. I was nervous because I hated hospitals. I thought about the people who had died, and those who were suffering on the floors above me. This awareness freaked me out. When I was at that hospital, I thought about what it must have been like on the day I was born in 1982. My mom told me that she smoked cigarettes in her hospital room after my delivery. I allowed my mind to wander while waiting for the technician to come into the room, and when she arrived, she made small talk as she squirted warm gel on me and began to roll the wand on my pelvis.

I stared at the monitor, hoping she didn't find a humongous tumor, but then I saw something on the screen. It was a tiny baby. It wasn't the bean-looking sac that I remembered seeing when I was seventeen and pregnant. This was an actual baby. I cried, and I couldn't believe what I was witnessing. There was no question of whether I would have this baby. It was a miracle.

The technician was as surprised as I was. "Looks like you didn't have a miscarriage after all!"

"How could this be? I've bled the past few months…"

"It's rare, but it happens. Your baby is alive and seems to be doing very well, but you'll have to follow up with your local OB-GYN when you get home."

Feeling overwhelmed, I remembered my lifestyle over the last two months and felt I had to be honest. "I didn't know I was pregnant. I've been partying. Will it be okay?"

"It's early; you and the baby should be just fine."

Relieved but still skeptical, I hoped she was right.

I couldn't believe this was happening. Seeing the shape of the baby on the screen, hearing the heartbeat, and witnessing the life within me that I thought had ended made me realize it was determined to survive. I recognized something special happening, though I couldn't understand why my fears had changed.

I stared at the screen with an overwhelming sense of peace that I didn't understand. I just knew that this baby was meant for me. No matter what was to come for us, I was going to make it work.

CHAPTER 17

My biggest fear was putting a child through what I went through as a child. I recalled the pain of being raised by parents who wanted to kill one another and nearly did at times—or worse, parents who almost killed themselves. I felt I had a pit in my stomach at night wondering about my parents and recalling wanting to ask them, *If you love me, why won't you stop hurting me?* I promised myself as a little girl I would never allow my child to feel that same way. Maybe that's why I thought I'd never have kids, but here I was pregnant, selling drugs, flying cocaine across the continent, and living with someone who attempted to control me. Yet, I had a sense of resolve that I would figure it out.

The hardest part for me was sobriety. I was miserable in my sober state. I felt depressed and the truth seemed magnified.

Luckily, I was too sick to want to drink so this helped me through. The problem with sobriety was that I could no longer hide from what was truly happening in my life.

I didn't want to fly back east to work after I learned about the pregnancy. I told Dean that I was worried I'd be one of the women who, after getting arrested, would be forced to give my baby up at birth while serving time in prison for federal drug charges. He wasn't ready for me to stop just yet. I was generating the most income between us, so in his mind, I had to continue. He didn't give me an option, and this is where I saw the significant shift in power. I felt more trapped than ever. He was well aware of my fears and how I felt about having to go back home, and he manipulated me using those fears.

I knew I had no real choice; I either had to leave him, in which case, I had nowhere to go, or suck it up and pray that all would go well on the next flight. I packed my stuff, resenting that I was doing something so risky for someone who supposedly loved me. I questioned this idea of love, and it made me realize I wanted to get far away from him.

As I walked through security with the Ziploc bag pressed against my belly, it clicked for me. He didn't care. To an outsider, his selfishness was obvious, I'm sure. With my distorted perception, I rationalized his behavior. I knew his past. He was also neglected and suffered worse abuse than I. I felt for him and granted him passes for behavior because I loved him. My time at the airport that day was clarifying. I didn't feel alone anymore, I knew I was here to care for someone else, and now he was getting in the way of that. I recognized that the runs were no longer for our family; he was being greedy. It felt like too much to risk in my situation. It was no longer worth it to me to take those trips. I heard Dean lecturing me, "You want nice things, but you don't want to put in the work for it."

Fuck him, I thought, and the anger pushed me into warrior mode. *I'd show him*, I thought. Maybe he knew he'd pushed me this way, but his ways were pushing me into work and away from him.

Dean lit a fire within me to outsmart him and make an alternative move for my own well-being. Back in Pennsylvania, I allowed the fire to spark growth in our operation. There were two women who bought from me and sold to others. They dealt with small amounts, but nonetheless, they were down to make some money. I had a feeling they both would jump at the opportunity to make more money, especially if I supported them.

One of the women was my aunt, and the other was a friend. I sat with it, and the idea played out in my head. I wondered how to get the product to them, and then it hit me. I'd ship it. Suddenly I remembered the story of a friend mailing packages with ounces of weed and another of a guy who shipped crystal meth, but that one hadn't turned out so well. Open to trying it, I shared the idea with Dean, and he was into it.

The plan was for them to make the sales and deposit money into my accounts at the end of the week. We tested the idea while I was home, and Dean shipped four ounces to my grandmother's home. The next morning, I sat nervously, waiting for the white delivery truck to make its way to me. My grandmother sat in her favorite La-Z-Boy recliner, watching her soaps, and I was on the sofa, so I could see out to the street.

The tracking said arrival by ten a.m. It was 9:37 a.m., so my eyes were peeled. I wished I could have a mimosa to take the edge off, but I had to feel it all. Each minute passing felt like ten, giving my mind time to torture me with visions of the police running up on me as I signed for the package. I rehearsed what I would say in the interrogation. "I didn't know. I had nothing to do with this…Of course, I am going to sign for a package; I thought it was a gift." I shrugged the nonsensical imagery away as I realized it sounded outrageous.

Peering at the grandfather clock across the room, the hand moved, and it was now 9:44 a.m. I heard the gears shifting of a loud vehicle. I jumped up and looked to the left where I heard the noise. I saw the white truck making its way to me.

"Oh, don't mind me. I have a package coming. It looks like it's here." I told my grandmom as I could see her concern when I hurried past her.

"Ah, okay. Good." She sipped her coffee and went back to the drama onscreen. *My poor grandmom,* I thought. *She'd possibly have a heart attack if she knew what I was waiting on.*

I hurried to the small foyer, standing behind the closed door, until the bell rang. The doorbell sounded, and I opened the blue door.

"Delivery for Nikki Sylvester," The delivery man said with an uninterested tone, which was a relief. I knew the plan had worked.

"Yes, this is she," I said, reaching for the yellow padded envelope.

"Sign here," he said as he chewed his gum.

I signed. "Thanks a lot."

Wow. *It's here. This changes everything.* At least, that's what I believed.

Even with two people on our team and our ability to ship, Dean still urged me to go to Pennsylvania myself. By then, he was out six nights a week while my belly was growing. I wanted him to visit with me and show him my life back East, but he was against it. He saw it as a waste of money and energy. "We are both handling business. That's how it should be. Leave the travel for later," he'd say.

He wanted me in Pennsylvania to keep an eye on what was happening, I felt like I was being pushed away on purpose. When I was in Vegas, I wanted attention. I wanted to play house to pretend that we weren't selling drugs and had a normal life. I wanted to be two excited parents who were expecting a baby.

I was on his ass about spending time with me, so we'd go to dinner at my favorite restaurant: N9NE Steakhouse at the Palms, but right after our dinner, he would drop me off at home and head out to make his runs. Most nights, he returned before six a.m. I couldn't sleep once I woke up after four a.m. and realized he wasn't home. Something told me he was with another woman, but I didn't want to believe it. I needed our family; I refused to be a single mother.

I had become accustomed to staying up waiting for his return. In the morning, I could gauge the time by the sun rising on the mountains. My bedroom window faced west with a view of the Summerlin mountain range. Even in my emotional turmoil, I could appreciate the beauty of the view. The sun rising in the east lit up the ridges in the most beautiful way. I often wondered what life in Vegas would be like if I chose to tough it out with Tonya. The reality is that one single choice changes everything forever.

One particular morning, I awoke and watched the mountain until seven a.m. I checked my phone—nothing. *What the fuck.* Sitting up and staring at the mountains, I felt the dread of facing Dean's betrayal. That morning, I just knew he was cheating on me. My rationalizing mind gave up and obeyed my heart. The tiny flutter of the kicking reminded me I was no longer alone in this; I needed to be stronger.

I called Dean; his phone was off. I tried again and again. Nothing.

Finally, his phone was back on and ringing. *Oh, I am so fucking done.*

I was blowing up his phone and screaming on his voicemail.

By nine thirty a.m. I was up in my bed. My eyes were swollen from crying. I had fully accepted that I was being cheated on.

The sound of the garage door opening startled me. I got up to walk downstairs to see what happened.

He stood at the bottom of the stairs; it was clear he was angry. I saw his face; he wasn't apologetic. Out of fear, I changed my tune. "I was so worried about you!"

Hesitantly, I walked down the stairs. He didn't blink; he didn't speak.

As I reached the bottom of the stairs, he slapped me down to the ground.

"Who the fuck you think you're calling twenty times? Don't you ever call me like that!"

I fell into fetal position and cried as I apologized. "I'm sorry! I was worried about you. I thought something happened to you."

He stood over me, listening to me apologize, I braced myself as he kicked me in my lower back. I cried out and lay there on the cool tile floor, protecting my belly. He turned to leave me there. He went upstairs, slamming the bedroom door behind him.

Crushed, I laid in that position for a few minutes after he was gone, I couldn't stop crying. My heart was broken. I didn't want this to be my life. I felt the flutters in my belly again, and I knew the baby was alive in there. The tears streamed down my cheeks, and I felt the pain of now living as my mother did. I loved someone who hurt me, someone who was also the father of my child. While I didn't know my baby, I felt its pain already, knowing it would be born into this. I promised the baby that we would be okay. When I made the promise, a surge of relief flowed through me, and I knew I had to leave Vegas.

When I sensed Dean was asleep, I crept upstairs to find out if he was asleep. Tiptoeing slowly on the carpet, I listened for him. As I neared the bedroom door, I could hear him snoring. I knew that drunk snore; I could sneak out. I grabbed whatever clothes were on top of the dryer, a stack of money from the kitchen cabinet, and ran outside to the edge of our community where I waited for a cab. I knew if he found me, there would be consequences. I was paranoid and hid between homes as cars drove by until my cab pulled up for me. I thought about what happened with Robert years ago, and I feared Dean would beat the cab driver or snap and run us off the road if he saw me. He wasn't himself that morning. When I finally reached the airport, I breathed a bit easier. Once I made it through security, I knew I was safe.

CHAPTER 18

I t hadn't been two hours since my plane landed in Philadelphia, and Dean was blowing up my phone with texts and calls. I was so happy to be away from him. I was safe to feel angry and hurt and not have to hide it to avoid his backlash. I was glad he had no idea where I would be. After the past few months of feeling like I was the one waiting and wanting, I was delighted every time my phone lit up with his attempt to reach me.

Good, I thought, *now you know how I felt, asshole.* Still tender from what happened, I didn't want to deal with Dean or his bullshit. I was consumed by emotion, yet I was too ashamed to tell my family the details, so I shared that we got into a nasty argument without the climax of me on the floor.

During the conversations with family and friends, I grieved for the baby on its way into our world. I had a broken family that I didn't know how to fix. I didn't have a safe space.

While I was home, I felt great for nearly forty-eight hours, then chaos ensued. Generally speaking, my family fought to the point that they became physical and started breaking things, and the police came. We loved each other, yet we never learned to deal with the pain we collected during our time together. In leaving home and coming back, I saw how hard some of us tried. We craved connection, but we weren't sure how to handle intimacy and feelings. Chaos was our set point, so we found our way back time and time again, no matter how badly it hurt us. My grandmother was an exception to this; she was the sweetest woman and avoided altercations at all cost. She did everything for all of us, yet, maybe for this reason, she was abused the most of all of us. Her children knew that she would bend, and since she didn't fight back, she was an easy target for them to place their pain and blame. My aunt lived with my grandmother, and she began giving my grandmother grief. They fought about everything. For example, my aunt and mother fought over who received more support from my grandmother over the years, and my mother even became frustrated with me, stating that I was the favored grandchild. She put that heavy blame on me from an early age. Her beliefs were transferred to my brother and sister, who also began resenting me for it. I didn't do anything to deserve this resentment, but this scarceness of love in my family interactions was a common occurrence.

During bouts of rage, my parents would create narratives to set my siblings and me against one another. In the midst of a fight between my parents, they spread their anger to us. Often it was smoke and mirrors. My parents attempted to upset me as I worked to calm them down. Depending on our mood and what our relationship had been that week, my siblings and I would brush it off as bullshit or we'd then argue and say hurtful things to one another. Our relationships never quite recovered, yet we loved each other. It actually hurt all of us to continue this behavior. We fought with the people closest to us constantly, out of fear, and this created major trust issues, which showed up in all of our lives. The whole "blood is thicker than water" analogy confused me most of my life. This turmoil made me miss my home in Las Vegas, where I only had to avoid one person's toxic behavior, and for some reason, it stung less when Dean hurt me.

When I left Vegas that morning, I was hoping this trip home would be different with my family; I needed it to be different for my own healing. It wasn't long before I realized it wasn't, and that didn't help me get over what was happening with Dean. He was calling every few hours, begging me to speak to him, but I refused to. Deep down, I wanted to speak to him. I wanted him to promise that it would never happen again and that he would go back to being the man he was when we first met. I wanted him to promise we'd live happily ever after. I knew that wasn't where we were anymore as a couple, but I did my best to make him sweat. Every four or five times he called, I'd answer just to tell him to fuck off or to tell him it was pointless to call until he wanted to tell me the truth. I was sick of the way he treated me. I knew there was something else happening between him and other women. I wanted to blame the women for the way he treated me; I was that far gone into delusion.

Four days into my stay in Pennsylvania, I had a nagging feeling that I was being betrayed. I became obsessed with finding the truth. All the late nights he stayed out, all the times my phone calls were rejected, and all the glitter and makeup added up. His anger and unwillingness to hear my concerns were another determining factor that he was hiding. It blew my mind that Dean went from my best friend to my enemy within a few months time. The late nights replayed in my mind for the better part of the day, and then suddenly it hit me: check the phone records.

The phones were in my name, so I could see whom he'd been speaking to. I went online and printed out the last month of bills. I sat on the sofa when everyone was out of the house and began searching through the over thirty pages of calls. Then I saw something that seemed significant. It was a fifty-minute phone call to a Washington state phone number. My heart rate increased when I saw he called the same number again. They talked for ninety-three minutes. Then I noticed a pattern. This number was all over the phone records. Who was so important in his life that he would want to spend hours on the phone with her, especially from Washington? We were in Nevada, and he was from Wisconsin.

My blood was boiling. I fucking knew it.

I called him. "Who the fuck are you talking to from Washington?"

He laughed.

"Don't fucking play with me. Tell me who this is...now!"

"That Vic's cousin, Ty. We are talking about making moves up there."

"Don't bullshit me, Dean! Tell me who she is! Last chance to come clean before I call myself."

"I told you..."

I hung up on him. I had enough of his bullshit. I was pacing. I wanted to call, but I wasn't totally ready to hear who it was. I remembered the mysterious phone call he received with the Mariah Carey ringtone back when he first began behaving differently. Maybe this was her number and I was about to find out.

My heart beat out of my chest and my hands were shaky as I dialed the number. The phone rang and rang again. Then I heard her.

"Hey, this is Rosy. Leave a voicemail, and I'll get back to you".

My heart sank. I was right.

I left a voicemail. I needed to know more. "Hi, this is Nikki. Please call me at 555-6790" *Wow. Can't believe I just did that. I left my number for her.* I wondered what she looked like. Was she prettier than me? Did she have a nicer body? Bigger boobs? Did he love her? What about our baby?

As much as I was hurt, I was equally relieved that I had some truth now. He couldn't lie to me anymore. I paced around my mom's living room. I felt the adrenaline move through every part of me as my mind displayed images of Dean and another woman. I drank a glass of water in hopes of calming my nerves until, fifteen minutes later, my phone rang. It was her. *Holy shit.*

Panic set in, and my mind raced. My heart was beating rapidly, but I inhaled, deeply exhaled, and answered the phone.

I didn't know what to expect. I thought she could take his side or tell me to back off or simply be a bitch about everything, but she didn't do any of that. I wanted to hate her, but I didn't. I could see why Dean liked her.

She started off, "I'm glad you called me. I want to talk to you, woman to woman, and tell you the truth."

She explained that she and Dean met while she was working in Las Vegas on the weekends. She was a dancer at the Spearmint Rhino, which meant she had to be pretty. She would fly in and stay at hotels, and eventually, she began to stay with him at our townhouse in my bed.

This had been going on for three months, and she knew there was a woman in his life because one day she opened my closet and saw my belongings. Yet he told her we were having issues and were separating, so she believed him. She said that, more recently though, she noticed a *What to Expect When You Are Expecting* book under the bed. She wondered what was going on and was getting to the point where she was considering leaving him alone.

"I wasn't willing to share him. I didn't want to do this. I gave it one chance and invited him to Washington to meet my daughter, but he had no interest. Right then and there, I knew it wouldn't work."

We shared stories about our time with Dean; I told her I left because he hurt me. I gave her details, which she wasn't too surprised about.

She told me that she was also worried he may have a "crazy streak," too. After they were at dinner one night, they were disagreeing about where their relationship was headed, and he grabbed her arm tightly. Right there and then, she said she saw a threatening look in his eye that felt like a major red flag. She said she knew he wasn't going to leave me, and she was getting fed up.

After we exchanged stories and said our goodbyes, the strangest thing happened, I wished we could have remained friends. She had power that I didn't see in myself; she was willing to walk away. I envied that about her. It was bizarre to think this way. Something about her ability to hold that conversation with me, regardless of our mutual feelings for this man, reminded me that women could stick together and support one another. I was fascinated by this woman and her relationship with my man, so much so that I somehow released my anger at Dean for being with her.

A few minutes after Rosy, I texted Dean, and I told him I knew everything. I cursed him out and called him all sorts of names and did my best to spark pain in him because I wanted him to feel how I felt. I knew deep down that was impossible because he didn't care like I cared. I was pregnant with a growing belly, and I was still hurting from the betrayal of having been hit by him. Now I was smacked with the truth that he was having sex with some other woman—in my bed—for the past three months. Hate wasn't a strong enough word to describe what I felt.

The anger was a mask to what was really happening: my fear of abandonment. I felt disoriented in my own body, like I was trapped around people who didn't know how to love me. I was beginning to analyze my entire life. I was terrified by the realization that I was ending up like my mother. She had a man treating her this way too.

Of course, nothing was identical, but there were painful similarities.

After my discovery, I shared the news with my mom. While she was disappointed, she urged me to give Dean a chance since we had a baby on the way. "Everyone makes mistakes," she reminded me. My dad heard and went along with it as he believed I should return. They saw him as a savior in my life. In moments like these, I learned to distrust myself. I was hurting. All of this was a big deal to me. I was hurt, but my family reminded me to brush it off. As the days went on, the sting from his drunken outrage and decision to cheat were overcome by the desire to get out of my mom's house.

After two weeks of him urging me to come home, saying the sweet promises my soul craved, I agreed to return. While I was sleeping on my mom's sofa with my family nudging me in that direction, it made sense. With the fighting at my mom's place, I was willing to risk it and try again. I went back with the promise of creating the family Dean and I never had growing up. Dean came from a broken home, too. His mother abandoned him for periods of time, and he lived in homes where he had been abused both physically and emotionally. Now that I knew what was happening, it felt like a barrier dissolved, and our communication opened back up. He told me he wanted to be different. Deep down, I knew he meant it, but could he? The night before I departed back to Vegas, we shared our greatest fears and hopes, and we promised to never put our child through similar experiences. My grandfather gained control over his rage and my dad stopped being violent over time, and I believed Dean could, too. I resolved to move through this; we would be stronger together.

CHAPTER 19

Comforting promises, gorgeous gifts from the Gucci store, and my internal yearning to be loved by a man who didn't know how had led me back to Vegas. As the days went on, Dean and I reconnected, and slowly, my hope was renewed. Emotionally, I felt I had lived through a tornado; the winds had stopped, but it took time to clear the debris. I wondered if I'd ever feel 100 percent safe with him. I was willing to try for my family. We learned that we were having a baby girl, and I consumed myself with decorating her room in pink and white tulle.

Working hard to remain hopeful, yet my fears were becoming more prominent. My body was expanding, and my insecurities were growing. I no longer felt sexy, which didn't help with my insecurities as I worked to forgive cheating and betrayal. I was having regular panic attacks, and I woke up petrified; literally, I would wake up and couldn't move. I could see, but my body was paralyzed by the fear. It was the most bizarre phenomenon, and at eight months pregnant, I found myself in the midst of an existential crisis.

Sobriety and the stress of my circumstances had me afraid, and I felt like something bad was going to happen. In general, I was terrified of death and the impermanence of all living things. When I learned of the recent passing of my friend, Beth, my fears of dying were magnified. I felt unsettled over the realization that everyone I loved would eventually die, myself included. I'd also get caught in the trap of thinking no one really loved me and I was alone. This fear led to a depression, and I judged myself as I read the pregnancy magazines where the women were living the best time of their lives. *Really?* I thought. *I can't be the only one freaking out.* But I also realized not everyone felt alone as I did. I quietly dealt with my fears and worked on crafts for Gia's room until the day I was given a real problem to worry about.

I was sitting on the bed, propped up against pillows, and watching TV, during one of my rare moments of peace, when Dean burst into the room. The horrified look on his face led me to the worst case scenario. *Oh no, someone else died?*

He stood directly in front of me and said, "I have to tell you something."

His face was different; his eyes were wide, revealing worry.

He continued, "Listen. I don't want you to freak out."

Panicked, I jumped up to move to the bedroom window, "Please, Dean, I'm not ready for more stress right now." My face was close to the screen, desperate for air like a dog in the car. I wanted to leave, but I knew I couldn't.

I could feel my heart palpitate. I held my belly, reminding myself that my little girl was with me, I was afraid. I never saw him worry this way.

I wondered if he were sick. *Oh God, does he have HIV? He's been promiscuous. Maybe he killed someone? Maybe he had gotten another woman pregnant?* I didn't want to know. I didn't know how to deal with the anxious sensations in my body without alcohol or pills. I feared for my health.

He continued, "Sit down. I need to tell you this now."

I was shaking. He led me to sit on the bed. He held my shoulder, which grounded me a bit.

"Just relax, please. Look, do promise me you won't freak out?"

I can do this. I nodded

"This is going to sound crazy. I'm not Dean. My real name is Aaron."

I was stunned. Was I alive? Was this a dream? My fragile world was falling apart with each word he spoke. I listened as he continued.

"Before I came to Las Vegas, I lived in Mazatlan, Mexico for six months. I fled the US because I was set to go to prison for a crime I committed against my ex."

I was shocked, but I was strangely relieved that it wasn't the terminal illness or the murder I imagined.

"Do you remember the call with the Mariah Carey ringtone?"

"How could I forget? Yes." I stared at him, taking him in. I didn't know him, but I listened.

"That was a woman I dated. She helped me escape from Wisconsin. Funny enough, she was also a criminal defense attorney back home. She called me back that morning because she had helped me get this far, but when you and I met, I slowed communication, so I didn't answer her call. Today she called me again and told me there is a lead on my case. The authorities know I'm in Las Vegas."

He was afraid. Visibly shaken. "I'm not going back to jail."

"It's okay. You will get through this. We have the money to pay for an incredible attorney."

"No," he snapped back. "I'd rather die."

I took a deep breath and asked him what he did to get into so much trouble. He explained he had drug charges and assault charges. He and his girlfriend were in a nasty fight, and he hit her with a vase, so she went to the hospital and called the police.

I couldn't believe what I was hearing. I felt like I was living in a movie. Was this a prank? I was ready to snap out of it.

He went on to tell me an unbelievable story. When he arrived in Mazatlan, Mexico, he lived comfortably, but then he began to run out of money and had trouble making strong connections in Mexico. His last hope was to come to Las Vegas because it was a transient city with heavy drug usage.

True, I thought. My eyes were wide and waiting for the story to end, but there was more to tell.

He had two little girls with a woman who now lived in Florida. The little girls were nine and thirteen.

"I knew something was weird. I felt it. You haven't been surprised by the progress of this pregnancy."

I wanted to freak out. I was afraid. He was vulnerable, and I knew he would snap over any little thing. I had to watch it.

"You can't tell anyone about this. No one. I'm not playing around."

I felt like I was in a Lifetime movie with way too much drama.

"I told you because I wanted you to hear it from me, just in case something goes down."

My eight-month-pregnant belly and I were stuck in Las Vegas because no more flying was permitted, and here he was hitting me with this bomb, and I couldn't tell anyone any of it.

The heaviness of this secret felt like a kettlebell on my chest. I felt even more isolated, realizing with painful discomfort that my entire life was a lie, but I couldn't tell a soul. Even still, I wanted to get it out of me. The idea I had of the family we could become shattered into millions of pieces, and I knew in that moment I was going to raise my daughter alone. We couldn't fix *this*.

I was afraid, which was typical, but now he was afraid, too. I went into supportive mode.

"Don't worry. Everything will work out. I'm here for you."

I said it, but I didn't believe it. It was a defense mechanism to keep myself safe, which was what I thought I was doing, but the voice inside my head said *runaway*.

My due date was 366 days after I first arrived in Las Vegas and unexpectedly met my daughter's father. A lot had happened in one year, and none of it was planned. It felt like years had passed since that evening when I rolled my luggage up to the island lounge, distraught and preparing to fly back to Pennsylvania.

In exactly one year, I found myself in a relationship with someone who was living a lie, and now I was completely sucked in. Our drug dealing operation was growing as fast as our problems were. We had placed a six-figure deposit on a home we were investing in—which was being built in my name—while I was aiding and abetting a wanted felon. I had a lot on my plate, but my number one concern was the baby. How would I find my way out of this?

CHAPTER 20

Dean and I celebrated our first anniversary on September eighth. Our baby, Gia Sylvester, was born on September 9th. There are no coincidences, yet it was bizarre to consider what had transpired in just one year. My mother and father who had never flown on an airplane in their lives willingly hopped on a flight when they found out I was in labor. I had never been so happy to see them. Watching the two of them with their first grandchild was heartwarming. I saw them differently. I hadn't seen them this way before. I knew the baby would change their lives, too. In fact, she already had.

While Gia changed the dynamic between my parents and me, it didn't have the same effect on Dean and I. We pulled up to our townhome from the hospital with our baby in tow. I was still sore from delivering her. Ninety minutes of pushing led to the Doctor using a vacuum, and I wound up with many stitches. The doctor advised me not to lift anything. I didn't think that would be a problem—until it became clear it was.

I got out of the passenger side of the car and looked back at Gia's face. She was so sweet; she fell asleep during the fifteen-minute drive. I admired her face as I looked to Dean, expecting him to pick up the carrier and bring her in.

He looked at me. "What are you waiting for?"

Feeling slow, I processed what he was asking me to do. "Oh, I didn't want to lift that because it's too heavy with my stitches."

"No, you're going to do it. Pick her up."

Stunned by the sharpness of his tone, the hurt welled up inside of me. I looked behind the car, hoping my dad would pull up and take over.

"Now." He peered at me. His tone was familiar; it was a warning.

My throat tightened as I held back tears. The tears would only piss him off more. I opened the door to the back seat and felt the pressure as I bent myself to reach the middle of his Dodge Charger. I unlatched the car seat and lifted the baby carrier, my stitches pressed up against the adult diaper the nurse instructed me to wear. *I hate him. I hate him. I hate him.* I silently affirmed my truth as I got her out and placed the seat on the ground to take a break.

Dean was already in the house as I lifted her up once more to head inside. She opened her eyes and looked at me. I met her eyes for a moment and reminded myself we needed to get away from this.

Walking in the house, I stopped as I heard, "Wait, Nikki!'

My dad pulled up without properly parking and hopped out to help. "What are you doing? You're not supposed to lift this."

"I know. I told him." Throwing Dean under the bus like he was my little brother; I was fed up.

My dad sighed and took Gia inside. I followed him in; my mom came in a few minutes after. I watched Dean gather his things and head out. I knew I wouldn't see him for hours. I was relieved. I wished my parents could stay this way forever.

Life went on and as our baby grew and so did my anxiety. Only I knew who Dean truly was. The secrets of his identity that weighed me down, yet I couldn't share with anyone. I wanted to tell someone and get it out, *I've been lied to and I feel lost.* I wanted to scream out for help and to declare that I found myself in deep shit and I didn't know how to get out of this. I was too afraid of what would happen if I did share and he found out, so I remained silent and went along with what Dean wanted to avoid further friction. Just before Gia was born, we placed a $136,000 deposit down on a new home being built on a golf course. We had to jump through a lot of hoops to buy the home with our illegal career; however, it was possible. Nearly anyone could buy a home in 2006—this was before the housing market crash. We opened a residential cleaning business front, had our attorney draw up a corporation, and created the backstory required to purchase the home. Our home was being built, which gave us time to filter income into my bank accounts. Everything was in place. We went together to choose our flooring, lighting fixtures, granite, and cabinets. I would daydream about things changing: opening a legal business and raising a happy and healthy little girl. Dean would realize he needed help, and everything would be solved. We'd heal together. This dream I had for my child was similar to the one I had for myself when I was waiting for my dad to change and get sober. Now I was waiting for my daughter's father to change. Would I spend the rest of my life waiting for a man to change?

Our home was situated on the seventeenth hole, and it was stunning. The Las Vegas real estate market was booming, and while I was uncomfortable with purchasing a $900K home in my name, I said yes. I felt I had the equity of the home to fall back on; only I would have access to this money as the owner.

While the sparkle of the new place lit us up for a few days, it was short lived as tension in our home became palpable. Within a matter of weeks, the joy of new rooms filled with beautiful new furnishings began to dim as negative associations were made. The move was the ultimate reality check for me. If we couldn't be happy in this beautiful environment, we never could. While it was amazing that two poor kids—who grew up in highly dysfunctional families with no real education—moved into this three-story home behind the green of the seventeenth hole. I was only twenty-four years old. I was naïve, hoping for better, as I dug my hole deeper. Dean was more stressed than ever. The money needed to furnish our massive new home combined with a losing streak with his sports gambling habit, led to an increase in Dean's aggression. I fed myself a combination of Valium, alcohol, and cocaine to manage my existence, but I pretended to be sober when I was around him. I don't know if Dean actually believed I was sober or he simply didn't care enough to say anything. My big home seemed to magnify my loneliness, and I was spiraling downward fast.

Within a short matter of weeks after giving birth, my life was complete chaos. The internal conflict of needing to be numb but also be a mother was overwhelming and painful. Every day seemed to tack on more guilt and shame. I was a high-functioning addict. I used the three substances together to get through my days. It was my way of feeling normal. I knew I was going to stop eventually. I promised myself that I would quit once things got better, once we stopped this lifestyle, once Dean calmed down, but soon that excuse shifted to as soon as I moved out on my own.

The first year of motherhood was a messy blur: a frightening, emotionally charged blur. The only thing that kept me grounded when it felt like I couldn't go on was my daughter. She was a mirror. She loved me, not just in a way that babies do, but she seemed to soothe me. When I was hurting, physically and emotionally, she seemed to reach for me. It was as if she could sense all of it and intended on making it better. She was the only person to love me so fully and never hurt me. Her love and her innocence kept me going; it kept me alive. Alone with the baby and with all the secrets I hid, she was my only light. The isolating lifestyle was excruciating, yet I didn't tell anyone because I didn't know what would happen. I'd think about Dean's other children and their mom, wherever they were. He had no contact with them, and here I was with his other baby. The images of abandoned little girls missing their father replayed again and again in my mind. I wondered if he would do this to our baby. What made us different? I had nightmares of the police storming into our home to arrest Dean and finding the kitchen cabinets were filled with cocaine, scales, and other paraphernalia. I was living in an emotional prison that only I could see, and the invisible bars were closing in on me.

Dean came home to eat and then went back out to hustle. He had become more aggressive, which led me to become more quiet and small. I was grateful for Gia. She barely cried; she was so well behaved. Her eyes would meet mine, and I felt that she could see into my soul. She knew what I needed. It was as if she knew that I was afraid, and her eyes said, "Don't worry. You can do this." Every time her father hurt me, I just held her, and she didn't make a sound. I promised her that we'd be safe and that I'd leave one day soon.

Dean's aggression led to more bruises, swollen lips, and the occasional black eye. I had invested in heavy-duty concealer and powders to hide my truth. While he was becoming more aggressive, I saw it as nothing deadly. My mom had black eyes before and so did my aunt. I decided I'd be okay.

This changed when Dean came home with his new gun. I was terrified, even just by looking at that weapon. Let's be clear, that man scared the shit out of me most of the time. I knew how to stay in line to keep the peace 95 percent of the time, but I was afraid of Dean without weapons. The idea of a pistol in my home was nightmarish. He told me the gun was purchased from Vic, his supplier. I hadn't been a fan of Vic, but this was the final straw. Dean would come home from Vic's office, which was in a strip mall near the strip. Here they played pool and drank Cognac while waiting on their next customer to text. Vic was also a pimp; his girlfriend was one of his "ladies of the streets," as Dean called them. While I was irritated by his fascination with this lifestyle, I wasn't surprised.

Dean loved his gun like a little boy with his first toy pistol on Christmas. He knew I was uncomfortable with his decision, but that didn't matter. A few weeks later, he returned home with a bigger gun, a TEC-9, and my fears skyrocketed. These guns triggered me; I had shot a gun before with friends on the train tracks due to peer pressure. I was too insecure to say, "I'm scared," so I did it once and went home as soon as I could. When I was sixteen, my cousin Brady went out with friends to rob someone in desperation to get high; they were addicted to smoking crack cocaine. That night, the gun was supposed to be there just to scare the victim, but instead, an innocent man—a father—lost his life that night. It was heartbreaking, and since then, I had never trusted aggressive people with guns. I had a fear they could go too far.

After being on the receiving end of Dean's anger, I didn't like the idea of guns being so close. I wanted to pretend the weapons weren't around, but he made it hard for me. Though we had separate cars, he'd still drive mine, and when he did, he'd leave a gun under the seat. When I sat in the driver's seat and adjust the settings, I'd feel the gun underneath my seat. I would curse him out in the privacy of the car and then carry the pistol inside silently. Before placing the gun in the cabinet, I'd carefully wipe my fingerprints off with a Clorox wet wipe. All of this happened while my daughter waited peacefully in her car seat. Gia was patient and quiet, always. It was as if she understood my pain and knew what I needed.

Dean didn't stop at the guns. He wanted to sell even more drugs than before. He added crystal meth and ecstasy pills to our services, which increased revenue quickly. Crystal meth was a big money maker back in Pennsylvania. No one we knew had access to the clear quality that we were supplying, and the profit margin was greater for our stuff. I'd been calculating our profits and plotting ways to escape and survive long-term, but I wasn't ready yet. By this point, I had stopped urging him to focus on a legal business; I was more focused on how I could get out on my own and get sober. To a sober woman who knows her worth, this is no big deal, but to a woman who had been neglected and abused her entire life, leaving the abusive man and getting sober was like climbing Mount Everest without shoes. It felt insurmountable.

Silently, I struggled with the shame that I wasn't ready to leave him. I'd heard both men and women say things like, "It's easy to leave. You just walk out of the door." Here's what those people did not understand about living in an abusive relationship: the victim also abuses herself. The person being actively abused already feels that she is unworthy or incapable of life alone. She is also afraid of what would happen if she were to leave. Would there be revenge? Would they make it to long-term freedom? After what happened with my ex-boyfriend Robert, I feared leaving. I was proud of myself for leaving Robert, and then weeks later, he kidnapped me and nearly killed me. After something like that happened, I began to think the safest and easiest choice was to work it out.

How was I to work it out though? My strategy was to work on

myself and learn to tone down talking back and defending myself, to become more of a "yes, honey" woman. I worked to try to stop caring about his cheating with the other women. Condoms were in his car and makeup on his clothing, but I was checked out by this point. It hurt, but I was beyond hoping he would change. I tried to ignore the fact that he would go out and have sex with someone only to come home and force himself into me at four a.m. when I was asleep. When he wanted something, he didn't give a damn if I had to wake up with our daughter in a few hours.

One morning, he came into the bedroom at five thirty. The sky was still dark gray, and he was obviously drunk. He came into bed, and I pretended to sleep, but that didn't matter to him. He reeked of cigarettes and Hennessy. The smells woke me even more, and he felt dirty on my skin. He was initiating sex with me, and though I didn't want it, that made no difference. I pretended to sleep, but it didn't matter; I had no choice but to go along with it so he would go to sleep and leave me the hell alone. Perhaps the most disgusting feeling in the world is to have someone inside of you that is unwanted and doesn't have permission, but you have no power to stop him. This became my normal. I did my best to tune out what was happening: to not feel and to leave my body. That morning, I reached a new level of disgust and decided I had to leave him soon. When he rolled over to go to sleep, the sky was pinkish-gray, and the sun was rising. I lay in the bed, feeling disgusted. I wanted to wash him off me. Waiting for his snoring to become steady, I found his clothing piled up next to the sofa where he must've stripped down before coming upstairs to disturb me. I picked up his pants and looked through his pockets where I found crumpled receipts and a hotel room keycard and condoms. I stood there at six thirty a.m., alone, and cried tears of overwhelming defeat. My body was weak from my daily routine of becoming numb. I needed sleep, but I couldn't find comfort in that now. The painful truths about my life that I had stuffed down were suddenly coming to the surface. The overwhelming anxiety moved through my body, and I felt a pang of loneliness that compelled me to reach out for help.

I wondered if I was being dramatic. I'd kept the secrets for so long. Was I in my right mind to share this information with someone? Searching for my phone, I saw it on the kitchen counter. Almost manic, I picked it up, scrolling through the names and wondering whom I could call. Who was safe on this list? As I stood there nervously, I pulled the Pinot Grigio from the fridge and filled a glass tumbler. Finishing the glass in two long sips, it dawned on me that none of my close friends felt safe. I judged myself. Was I being paranoid? But then it hit me—my friend's girlfriend, Ella. Yes, she felt like she could handle this. She could handle me.

I filled my glass once more, feeling the warmth of my first drink setting in. Opening the kitchen cabinet, I used the tip of a butter knife to scoop a small amount of cocaine and placed it directly under my nose and sniffed it up quickly. I felt the familiar surge of adrenaline, and then I knew I could do this. This was my morning coffee. I was now ready for the vulnerability required to make this call.

Picking my phone up once more to look for her name, I realized I didn't have her number. *Fuck.* I did have my friend's number, so I texted him. "Hi. Will you send me Ella's number? I have to ask her something, and it's really important."

Within two minutes, he texted me back. "Sure. Is everything okay?"

I felt the shame of my reality set in for a moment. *Does he sense what is going on?*

I decided it didn't matter as I responded, "Yes, everything is fine. Just want her opinion."

Finally, I had her number, and I dialed it. Waiting for her to answer, I flashbacked to the last time I saw her at my baby shower. My mom threw me a gorgeous baby shower; she surprised me with what she put into it. Ella came with my friend. We didn't speak much, but I knew her background of abuse and addiction from nights we were up late partying. She wasn't new to suffering; she'd shared a lot of what she felt as she shared the heartbreaking story about her stillborn daughter. In fact, I thought of her and her baby often when I was pregnant, but I didn't share my fears with her. There was something about her energy that told me she was the person to call, even though logically it didn't make sense.

She answered, "Hello?"

"Hi, Ella. It's Nikki. Can you talk?" I tried to sound normal, but I wasn't doing great.

"Hey, yes, I can. Are you okay?" I sensed she didn't feel bothered by my call so I moved into my laundry room, shut the door behind me, and sat on the floor.

I took a deep breath and let it out. "No, I'm not, and I haven't been for a while. I don't know where to begin...Okay, you know Gia's father, Dean?"

"Of course."

My heart was racing. I was paranoid. What if he could hear me from upstairs? I kept going.

"He's not who he said he was. In so many ways. For one, he's been hitting me and cheating on me." Saying that out loud made me cry. "What's been eating away at me worse is that his real name isn't Dean. He lied; he has an entirely different life. He's currently on the run. He is facing a lot of time."

As I paused, crying and feeling the release of letting someone else in, she interjected.

"Oh, Nikki! Where is Gia?"

"She's upstairs, still asleep. I'm exhausted. I barely slept, and he came home and forced me away. I saw that he was with another woman, and I just can't take much more of this. I don't know what to do. I'm scared to leave."

As she listened, I felt a shift in myself. She and I brainstormed ways to leave and stay safe. Imagining what it would be like to leave gave me a bit of hope. We talked for ninety minutes until Gia woke up. She promised not to tell a soul. I just hoped that I made the right decision, and I knew that only time would reveal whether I made a wise choice.

Ella wasn't the only person I cried to for help. The next call was a week later and harder to make, even though I had known this person my entire life—my dad. I didn't plan to call him, but I found myself in a dark place at four a.m. when I was about to polish off the remainder of the Pinot Grigio bottle. My eyes hurt from the brightly lit computer monitor. I sat staring at the screen while berating myself. What kind of woman would deal with this? What kind of mom would do this? I had a daughter, and I promised myself that my child would have a different childhood experience. I was a liar. *A weak, pathetic liar*, I thought. I hated myself. The voices in my head were nastier than ever. That night, I worried I may not make it with the internal noise. The nights at the desk alone became my ritual. The baby would sleep, and I would escape myself. The internet was my best friend as I searched for rehabilitation centers, therapy, and life coaches that could help with addiction and trauma. I was scared I'd never get away from the life I was living. I didn't want to be high or drunk; I wanted to feel good and be a good mom.

I kept telling myself that if I could just get through tonight, I'd feel stronger tomorrow. After months of getting through one more night, I wondered how many nights I truly had.

Calling my father, I knew he could understand since he struggled with addiction. We never talked about feelings or fears. We remained on the surface at all times. I felt raw; I didn't know who else to call for solid advice. I needed someone who knew what it would take for me.

Crying, I spoke to him: "Dad…I'm worried."

"What's wrong?" He sounded casual, yet I could sense his concern.

"I don't know if I can stop doing what I am doing." I was unsure if I could admit what I was *doing* out loud. But he knew; they all knew. They knew how we made money, and they knew I was on drugs, but it had been the norm for all of us in our own ways. No one resisted it. It was just how we were.

"I'm wondering if I need rehab. I don't feel well; I don't know what to do." My voice was shaky as I decided to tiptoe around what I really felt. I couldn't find the courage to share that I was scared these voices in my head would lead me to my own death.

Frustrated by the intimacy of this conversation, he replied, "Nik, you don't need rehab. You need to get your shit together and worry about the baby. Just do it. You don't need someone else to help you."

My throat tightened, and the tears followed as my one potential guide was checking out.

"Okay, Dad. I know. I'm gonna go." I cut him off because I needed to cry, knowing he didn't want to hear it.

"Alright."

I put the phone down and sobbed until clarity came. I knew that I needed to get sober to live on my own with Gia. I knew, deep down, that I could do it on my own. My dad went to rehab, and it didn't work; he finally got sober on his own; I could do it too. I had to. Or I wouldn't make it. The demons in my mind were leading me to places I didn't want to go. I knew Gia needed me. I had to do this for her.

CHAPTER 21

Gia's cry signaled it was time to start the day, I reached for my phone to check the time; it was 8:05 a.m. I got up and went into Gia's room to find her sitting up in her crib, happy to see me. I carried her downstairs where Dean was sleeping on the sofa. As I prepared Gia's breakfast, she was playing on the living room floor with her wood blocks. Dean was irritated that we were being loud, but I didn't care. I was being loud on purpose since I felt he should be up with us.

I had only slept four hours myself, yet I was up doing what needed to be done, and I was fed up with him. His selfish ways were driving me insane. He was going out with other women, bossing me around and treating me as if I were worthless. He started comparing me to his mother and the way she cleaned the house and cooked. *Fuck you*, I thought. *Your mother who supposedly abused you? Please don't even go there.*

The dishes shifted in the sink, causing a loud clanking sound, and he jumped up and yelled at me. "You had to wake me up, didn't you?" He was pissed and extra cranky due to a hangover and lack of sleep. "Make me something to eat." His tone pierced me. I could feel anger radiating through my body as I went on to prepare a plate of food for him. Less than ten minutes later, he summoned me. "Get over here and change Gia's diaper."

I couldn't handle it anymore, and though I knew I was on thin ice, I couldn't suppress my voice.

"Really? You can't change it while I cook? She's right in front of you," I replied.

"Change the fucking diaper and quit asking questions." His eyes told me not to say another word. I wanted to listen, and I knew I shouldn't say anything.

As I walked around the kitchen to get the wipes, I felt overcome by his violation. My voice was stifled for so long it felt like combustion. I mumbled, "I'm so sick of this." I knew it was too much. My body felt it; I went too far.

He stood up; Gia was still sitting on the sofa next to him. He reached down, grabbed Gia's wooden toy, and threw it at me. I attempted to cover my head, but it hit me hard. I looked down at the white ceramic tile and saw my blood. My head was numb, and I couldn't feel where he hit me. I was scared to see what was happening as the blood flowed onto my gray T-shirt. I tasted it as it hit my lips, and I was scared. Gia wasn't crying, but she was looking; she looked shocked as she leaned on the sofa, staring.

Dean pushed me and said, "You see what you did? You never learn to shut your fucking mouth, do you?"

He walked away and went up the stairs. Internally, I was frantic as the blood continued to stream down the sides of my cheeks and onto my clothes and the carpet. Gia was now in the kitchen, looking concerned. I knew she sensed that she shouldn't cry because it would add tension to the situation. I walked into the bathroom for a towel and carefully avoided the mirror. I was scared to look at what happened, and I thought I might freak out and lose more blood, so I held the gray towel to the top of my head and decided to go upstairs to check on Dean. I was worried he was upstairs to get one of his guns.

When I made it into our room, he was sitting upright on our bed. He didn't look concerned, rather his eyes told me he was still pissed. He was fed up with me, too, as if I were simply an irritation in his life. "You never know when to shut up. You never learn, do you?"

"I'm sorry! I'm not feeling well today. I couldn't sleep last night. I'm really sorry."

I wasn't sorry about what happened, but I needed to fix my bleeding wound. I needed to get to the hospital, and I knew he wouldn't let me drive nor would he let me leave with Gia. I had to get him to believe me that I wouldn't tell anyone what happened. "I'll work on it, I promise," I said with desperation in my voice. I wanted to live, and I wanted to get out of there.

"Dean, please. I gotta get stitches. Please drop me off at the hospital. It won't take long, I promise."

He glared at me, as if he were disgusted by even the sound of my voice. I could tell I was inconveniencing him. He thought I was pathetic, which I was. I was there begging a man to forgive me when he was the one who needed to ask for forgiveness. I didn't care; I said whatever I needed to say to stay safe and make it through the situation. I was afraid and reverted to negotiation mode. I was panicking but attempting to play it cool. I knew he would take me if I was grounded and calm or else someone may find out what happened. Pulling myself together with each breath, I felt the blood soaking through the hand towel.

"Dean, I need to fix this. No one will know what happened. I'll say something fell on me in the garage. Please, I want to fix this. I'll call you when I'm done, and I'll come home to clean this mess."

I could tell I was getting through to him. "When I get home, I'll clean up, and we can work this out. It will be better. I promise."

Gia was on my hip, and I held her with one arm as I used my left hand to press the towel to my scalp. My head was throbbing now that the adrenaline levels had lowered

"Please, Dean…"

When he got up off the bed, my heart skipped, and again the adrenaline pumped through my body as he walked toward me.

"Let's go…now."

A wave of relief moved through me. I would get through this. This wasn't the end.

I looked at Gia and wondered what she was thinking there with her sweet, chubby cheeks, looking so calm. I don't think she understood, but she kept me together during times like that. She didn't deserve it. I knew that and so did Dean. When he was sober and clear-minded, he wanted the best for her. Dean definitely didn't want Gia to lose her mom, but the demons inside of his head were getting louder.

We arriving at the hospital where Gia was born, and I walked into the ER where I was taken to the back within minutes. I had a splitting headache, and I worried I had a concussion—or worse—that I was dying. The nurses and physician questioned me, and I clearly and calmly explained that I was looking through boxes in the garage, and a shelf holding paint cans fell on my head. I wondered if they bought the story, but they didn't challenge me. I knew one of the nurses could tell I was being abused; she asked me more details when the doctor left, and she looked at me with empathy; I could feel it. I was scared, and people could feel the fear. I had to go back to my own personal hell after this hospital visit. If I had Gia with me at that moment, I wouldn't have gone back. I considered if I could ask the police to go back to the house with me. I doubted I had the guts to do that though. When he got out of jail again, I knew he would kill me, and I didn't want to live with that fear. Regardless, Dean was smart to keep Gia with him.

The results of my scan came back, and everything was clear, but there was a laceration on the crown of my head that needed ten staples. Then I'd be good to go.

After all that I went through, I couldn't believe I was still scared to get the staples since my head was already hurting. I wished I wasn't alone in the room; I wanted someone to hold me and give me strength. I was waiting for the pain meds to kick in, and they numbed me a bit.

While I waited, I reminded myself to stay strong and to breathe. I was alive, so I could still do this. The worst was over.

Dean began texting me, and I could tell he was nervous. In that moment, I felt strong enough to leave him. If Gia was there with me, we would have escaped and never returned. Being there alone and afraid of getting those staples in my scalp made me realize that things had gone too far.

I told myself I would figure out my escape when things calmed down. Then I would escape for good. I lay in the hospital bed, enjoying those moments of safety before the nurse came with the discharge paperwork. Within an hour, I was back home with Gia and Dean.

In the days after the hospital visit, I was on my best behavior. I was cleaning the house, making beautiful meals, and staying super quiet. I didn't have anyone to tell besides Ella. She and I spoke almost daily when Dean left. She had become my saving grace and a voice of reason and support. My mom and dad would have flipped out if they knew; they would never support us staying at this point, but I knew they both had a temper, and I couldn't trust them not to call him and make matters worse. Unintentionally, they may get us hurt. Dean said many times, "I'm not going back to jail; I'd rather die." I imagined a standoff with the police where he killed all of us.

About a week later, I was healing nicely. I had a few more days to go before the staples would be removed. While my scalp was healing, my heart felt broken. I lost all hope for this man and my family. I was grieving the truth, and I began accepting that I was going to be a single mother and Gia wouldn't have a relationship with her father.

The first step of the plan was getting away from Dean. He wouldn't allow me to leave the house with Gia since the morning of the bloody incident. I had a flight scheduled for Pennsylvania in the coming week, and he already told me I wasn't taking Gia along. She never stayed alone with Dean, and it made me uncomfortable because he was always in his own world. I knew he would leave her in the crib alone to run and meet someone, and I worried what would happen if he got arrested or killed. My imagination spun out of control until the images made me feel sick, I had to I stop the toxic train of thought.

I had to go on the trip. He made that clear, and I was not going to fight too hard. I was too scared. Since that morning, I wasn't allowed to go anywhere, not even to the store. He took the keys to the other cars. Yet, I knew this couldn't go on forever. I felt he would give up on that level of control soon enough. He'd get comfortable, and then I could escape with Gia.

My time in Pennsylvania was short and sweet, but for a while, I was free again. While I was there, I visited apartment communities and prepared for our escape. I knew it was happening soon, but I wasn't sure when. Forty-eight hours later, and with $30,000 pressed on my body, I returned to Las Vegas. I had a car service pick me up, and my first stop was the casino where Dean had me bet on boxing matches to launder some of the money. I still didn't understand the money laundering strategy, but I didn't ask. My focus was on behaving submissively around him until I found my way out. Asking questions got me into trouble, so I just went ahead and did my job.

Opening my front door, something was odd. The entire house was spotless. Dean refused to invest in a cleaning service since he said I could do it. This seemed weird to me. When I walked into the kitchen, he was standing at the center island. He wanted to talk to me about what he had done around the house. I listened until it became clear that this dude did drugs. I couldn't believe it. I waited to see the truth with certainty, and I kept observing him as he talked. I knew the signs, but he was so against drugs, except for the occasional ecstasy. "Doing cocaine was for white boys," he'd say. Even though his mom was white, Polish American to be exact, and his dad was African American, Dean identified as Black. Yet, he had to be doing blow; it was apparent.

The possibility of him doing meth was unimaginable to me. I couldn't believe it was possible. I didn't want to accuse him of anything because that could backfire. The surprising thing was he was chipper and funny. I liked this friendly version of him. I listened closely, finding myself amused by him, but I still knew his temper and recognized that adding drugs to the mix could be a lethal combo if I tested him.

Gia was so happy to see me, and she looked well cared for, which made me feel good. Gia loved me, but she was a Daddy's girl, and he was a different man toward her. Bewildered by what I had walked into, I went upstairs to begin unpacking my stuff, and I started texting Ella about what was going on. I also decided to text my friend Michelle since her boyfriend, Curtis, hung out with Dean from time to time. She said Curtis went over to visit Dean, and he stayed up for two days straight.

Wow. My mind was blown by what was happening. In two years, he had never ever taken drugs...and now? I felt he was losing his shit. That was it. That was the end. He was already crazy, and I feared the drugs would take him over the edge.

I felt like I had to keep my composure once I knew he was high. He was also up my ass more than usual. Typically, he would drink and either slow down or go out, but now he was here with me, wide-awake. We got through the night somehow, and eventually he fell asleep. The next day, he woke up hungover and went right back to being down and short-tempered.

Reality was catching up with him. There was too much pressure to deal with and so much he was running from. He was juggling the fear of being caught by the Feds for the crime he committed in Wisconsin, grappling with the realization that he left his kids left behind, and dealing with the weight of the morning of the bloody incident. He finally fell into numbing himself with drugs, and I knew it would be hard to get out. I knew it firsthand. To make things worse, he had access to a nearly endless supply.

He was stuck on the sofa for the entire day. I knew the horrid feeling that came after riding a high for days only to experience the emotional crash back into depression when waking back up. I was in the kitchen, but I kept my eye on him in the living room since I didn't know what to expect from this man.

Then he called out for me. "Nikki, I want you to look up apartments in San Diego. I want us to move in two weeks. We need a change of pace."

My mind rejected this request. "Dean, we have our house here. Are you sure?"

His tone was harsh. "I'm not asking you. I'm telling you to find us a place. Do it."

I was startled by the tone of his voice. The man I knew wouldn't have done cocaine for two days and run off to San Diego. I wasn't willing to run away from our home with him. I didn't know anyone in San Diego, and I didn't want to go because I felt I would be trapped there alone with just Gia. The isolation of a move like that scared me. I wasn't willing.

Panicking, I felt like I was being kidnapped and imprisoned by him. I wasn't allowed to leave the home with Gia, but at least I had my home, and I felt comfortable in my surroundings. Now he wanted to take us to San Diego, and I felt overwhelmed when I thought of the work it would take to pack and move. I simply didn't have it in me to go along with his plan. I had to escape. "Okay, I'll look them up and show you my favorites. I'm going upstairs to research, okay?"

I took the laptop and made my way up to the third floor for privacy. I'd hear him if he was coming up there, so I felt safe to talk. The third floor consisted of one room with windows on every side. I sat on the small leather sofa, staring at the Vegas strip in the distance as I gathered my thoughts. I texted, Ella, "Please answer. It's urgent." Quickly, I dialed Ella, and she answered. I whispered, "Dean wants us to leave for San Diego. He's losing his shit here. I'm worried."

"I didn't tell you this because I didn't want to scare you, but you gotta leave."

Her words paralyzed me.

"I had a nightmare about your house; the police were there with a dead body. The nightmare happened two nights ago after you left."

She freaked me out, but I told her not to worry and that I was leaving. I would figure it out.

"Gotta go. Love you."

How can I get away before Dean forces me to leave for San Diego?

My mind moved one hundred miles per minute. Ella's dream frightened me because both she and I had premonitions about death. She dreamed that her doctor would tell her of her stillborn within two days of it happening. When I was fifteen, I had a dream that my grandmother was shopping for flower memorials for my grandfather. The dream disturbed me so much that I told my family the next day. That very next morning, a state trooper arrived at my Grandmother's to notify her that my grandfather was hit and killed. Now Ella's dream was like a fire beneath my feet; I had to get out.

I pulled up a page with a list of high-end apartment buildings in San Diego, and I went back downstairs where I stood at the kitchen island, calling out the locations and prices of each unit as I found them.

I could hear him mumbling something; it sounded like he was complaining about me. I was on the phone so I did my best to tune it out.

As soon as I hung up with the realtor, he yelled out for me.

"Make me something to eat."

How can this man eat right now? My nerves were shot and I felt like our life was completely was up in the air. I didn't know what the hell was happening.

"Okay."

I looked in the fridge, and I found pizza he must've purchased while I was away, so I pulled it out to reheat it. I realized my hands were shaky so I decided to take a Xanax. As I went to my bag to pull out the medicine bottle, it hit me: *I could leave right now.* My heart palpitated as I grasped what I was considering. I realized that I could put him to sleep with Xanax and leave with Gia. *Oh shit, I can do this,* I thought.

With the prescription bottle in my hand, I walked back to the pizza on the counter top. My mind was moving so quickly; I was worrying about money and making it to the airport. I thought I was going to have a heart attack while attempting to do this. If he caught me leaving him, he would no doubt beat me to death.

So much was at risk, and I was scared. I knew that things were spiraling out of control though, and I felt backed into a corner. I assessed the events that had been happening. It scared me to think of being caught by him. and Ella's nightmare came to mind. What if it was my body she saw in that dream?

Fuck it. I had to try. This was my chance. First, I needed the pill I took to begin to work and settle my nerves. I thought for a moment about what I'd take with me, but then I realized it didn't matter what I took along if I had enough money with me. I could buy everything I needed along the way as long I knew we were safe.

While I plotted my getaway, Dean was growing impatient.

"Where's my food?"

"It's coming. Sorry. I was deciding what to make."

As I plated two slices of pepperoni pizza and popped them in the toaster oven, the familiar, soothing feeling of that tiny blue pill came over me, working its magic in my bloodstream. It was time to get to work if I was going to do this. I had to give him enough to get him to fall asleep deeply, and since he was triple my size, I figured he would need much more than I took. Suddenly I worried if the hot food would interfere with the drug efficacy.

"Make me hot tea, too."

Perfect, I thought. *I'll add it to that, too.* I broke up one pill into his tea and added honey. I used a spoon to taste it. It was sweet enough that I couldn't taste a thing. I crushed another two pills on the granite countertop using the bottom of the tea mug. I looked into the living room to see if he was still sitting down, and he was. Next, I scattered the blue powder beneath the cheese on his slices of pizza. Luckily, though the pill was small, it packed a punch. This would do it as long as he consumed all of it.

I gathered all my strength to keep my hands steady as I handed him the plate. "Here you go. Tell me if you want more."

He wouldn't be able to tell the pills were in there. I knew that. I realized he had no clue what I was planning, and suddenly, I saw his innocence. Rather than feeling happy, I was hit with overwhelming with sadness for what I had done. But it was too late now. I watched him take his first bite, and I was overcome with guilt. Had I become just like him?

Images of our first meeting came to mind. I loved him then, but that version of Dean checked out over a year ago. It hurt me that it had come down to this, but I had to escape him. I wondered if I was being too dramatic, and I even judged myself as evil. There were so many moments when it seemed like I hated him, but I didn't. I just felt an intense hurt. It was the pain of being betrayed and hurt. Regardless, I loved him. I fell in love with someone who I thought was my best friend, and I wanted a happy life together with him where we could raise our child. I never wanted any of this. If he weren't keeping us as prisoners in the home, I wouldn't have to take such drastic measures.

As I watched him eat the pizza and take a long sip of the chamomile tea, I realized another woman would end up enjoying my house. I was leaving all my stuff behind and everything I had risked my life to build. I didn't want him with other women, and I didn't want other women in my home. Suddenly, I felt confused by my feelings, so I pushed the images out of my awareness and reminded myself I didn't want *this*. I wanted the version of the man that I met back in 2004, even though that man was long gone.

He finished and put his plate on the table beside the sofa. I quickly stood up to bring it to the kitchen. From there, I watched him as he was watched television. Gia was sitting between his legs, holding her favorite stuffed unicorn.

I took the bottle of Santa Margarita out of the fridge and took a long sip out of the bottle. Bracing myself for what I was about to do, I called upon all the courage I'd ever had. I thought back to the moments when I walked through TSA with a quarter kilogram of cocaine. If I could do that, I could do this. *Come on, Nikki!* I gave myself an encouraging pep talk. I knew I had to do this. Recalling every scary moment I had already pushed myself through, I told myself it was time for warrior mode.

About fifteen minutes later, Dean had peacefully dozed off. I gave it some more time before testing it out and calling him. "Dean."

Nothing. So, I ran upstairs to the laundry room and gathered some clean clothes for us and placed them in a bag. I ran downstairs and peeked into the living room to see that he didn't move. I went into the cabinet where he kept the money. I grabbed a stack, which I knew contained over $20,000, but I didn't take time to count since it felt like enough. I would make it work.

I walked back to the living room; I called his name: "Dean..."

Nothing.

A bit louder now. "Hey, Dean..."

No movement; he was out.

Though I was excited by the reality of my escape, I was also feeling like a piece of shit. I felt sad that I was leaving during a vulnerable time for him; I knew he had no one else. I was all he had, and now I was leaving him alone. As he lay there, I admired him, and I witnessed the truth that there was a scared little boy beneath his violence and anger and that part of him was in pain. Plus, he had his very own abandonment issues to deal with. But I had to do this because I was scared of him, and he was hurting me. I couldn't live like this anymore. Gia deserved better. Something bad was going to happen if I didn't leave. I would end up in jail or dead if I stayed. This was the best choice.

I stuffed the money in my black Gucci diaper bag. I also had my phone and charger with me. I opened the door and then the garage door to see if he would budge. Still nothing.

Sweat accumulated on my forehead. I felt hot and dizzy from the adrenaline rushing through me. I hurriedly buckled Gia in her car seat and then backed out of the driveway. I pressed the button to close the garage and sped out of the complex like I was running from the police.

I called my dad and asked him to book the next flight for us. I told him it was an emergency, and he could hear something was wrong when he heard the tone of my voice because he refrained from his sarcastic retort.

I knew I would come back and sell the car one day, which meant more money for me, so I decided to leave it on a residential street close to the airport. We caught a cab to the terminal, and once we moved through the airport security line, I knew we were safe. He wouldn't put himself at risk by coming there with all the police. He didn't call me, so I knew he wasn't awake yet.

I snuggled Gia as we sat at Chili's restaurant in our terminal. I couldn't believe I did it. I actually had the courage to leave him, and this time, I knew there was no returning.

CHAPTER 22

Within a week of my return to Pennsylvania, I moved into a new place, purchased a new car, and drank myself to sleep every night. The reality of my new life was sinking in, and it was hard to accept.

Why wasn't I celebrating? I escaped him, so why was I so sad? I hated myself for those feelings. I resented my depression. Ella reminded me that it was still too soon to expect things to feel right since I had just left. She encouraged me to give it time.

Being a single mom felt like the worst thing to me. I felt like I couldn't take care of myself, much less raising a daughter on my own. Dean always told me I wouldn't be able to raise Gia on my own, and he was probably right.

I'd look online at job openings for entry-level jobs during the day, and then I'd go out at night to forget it all. My parents were so happy Gia was nearby; they helped me a lot with her. One night after going to the bar, I was dropped off at my place, but I still couldn't sleep. I lay down in my bed in the dark when the phone lit up.

It was Dean. I didn't answer.

He called again.

Then he called four more times. Something told me to answer.

"What do you want, Dean?"

"Nikki, I just wanted to tell you that I love you, and tell Gia that I love her, too."

His voice startled me; something was off. He sounded different.

"What are you talking about? What's going on?" I heard loud noises in the background; I heard a woman.

"What the fuck, Dean? What the hell are you doing?" I was angry.

"You're not going to hear from me again. Remember what I said." I could hear sadness in his voice.

He hung up. I jumped out of bed and called him repeatedly. Nothing.

After ten minutes of trying to get through to him, I called Ella, and I asked her to try to call him, too. I told her something bizarre was happening with him. She tried calling him, too. No response. Eventually I went to sleep frustrated. *The nerve of him. After all he's done, he calls me like that?*

The next morning, I awoke with the same worries I had fallen asleep to. I wondered what happened that prompted him to call like that. I had a heavy feeling in the pit of my stomach. He didn't sound like himself when he called. Questions weighed on me as I waited for him to return my calls. Did he kill himself? Who was the woman? I didn't know what to think, and I was worried, but I told myself he would return my calls soon enough. I usually knew how to get a response from him, so I decided to send one more text.

Dean, if you don't return my call in three hours, I am sending the police there.

Hours later, still nothing.

When I called that night, his phone was off. This was a bad sign because he never turned his phone off. Money was number one to him, and so he would buy a new charger or a new phone or do whatever he needed to make sure he could make his connections. His phone wouldn't stay off for more than thirty minutes at a time.

I bought a case of Amstel light, and I found someone to buy a gram of cocaine from. I stayed up drinking and texting Dean through the night. As I got higher, I imagined that he was dead in our home, and I felt like I made a mistake by leaving him. I feared that it was the wrong decision to leave him since I knew he wasn't emotionally stable. But I did it anyway, and for those reasons, I sank into self-hatred and blame.

What if I did this? This wouldn't have happened if I didn't drug him and leave him alone. The inner battle continued. *But he hurt me. I was afraid. But still, I shouldn't have left him the way I did. I made it worse. He called to tell us he loved us. He always loved us. Maybe I was the problem.* I had the somewhat typical illusions of a manipulated woman who had been blamed for her own abuse for years.

Tears were streaming down my heated cheeks, and the cold beer soothed the metaphoric sharp ball of emotion in my throat. I called Ella, and she assured me that I didn't do this. She reminded me of the staples in my head less than two months ago. "Don't forget the black eyes you had to cover up!" She was right. "Nikki, he is his own person. You aren't responsible for him. You have to care of yourself and Gia." Yet, after another twenty-four hours with no word from Dean, I decided I must know what was happening. I considered calling the police, but I didn't know the ramifications of all the guns and drugs in my home. Would I be arrested, too? Without Dean to help me, how would I get out of prison if I did get arrested? I went to jail after a bar fight once. After I sat in jail for three days, Dean sent $15,000 to get me out. If I went to jail now, it would be for longer, and it wasn't worth the risk. The number of drugs and number of weapons in the house would result in them setting such a high bail that it would be beyond what my family could ever come up with.

I called my Las Vegas friends, and they hadn't heard anything either. One of them went by the house for me and saw no lights on. That night, I stayed up all night drinking Crown Royal alone, unable to shake the feeling that something bad had happened. I couldn't just sit there in Pennsylvania while Dean was dead or hurting at the house. Drunk and sitting alone in my new apartment at three a.m., I decided to book a flight back to Las Vegas in the morning. Ella agreed to travel with me. I planned to get the car, book a hotel room, and get to the bottom of whatever was happening at my house. I was afraid of what I'd find, but I felt relief in knowing I'd have an answer shortly. Every part of me screamed that there was a major problem.

The next morning, I was feeling hungover and groggy at the Philadelphia airport. As bad as I felt, I was ready to get some answers. Standing at the gate, waiting for boarding to begin, my phone rang. It was 702 number. Now he calls. *Finally*. I braced myself.

Fully prepared to curse him out for what he's put me through in the past few days, I answered, "Hello?"

"Hello, Nichole Sylvester?" an older man's voice said.

I hesitated and then replied, "This is she."

"This is Vegas Homicide. We are at your home here on Crooked Putter. We've found a dead woman in your home. We thought it may have been you, but apparently you're okay…"

My heart sank.

I felt the world around me stop. Everything in me rejected what I had just heard. *No, this is a dream; this isn't real.*

My knees were weak as I gasped for air.

"Who is she?" My mind was racing through the potential women. "Wait, where is Dean?"

"Aaron, you mean? We haven't found him yet, but the other two men who were at your home have given us the information we need to find him. We should have him soon," the man said. "The neighbors said they haven't seen you and your daughter lately. We need you to come out and claim your home. When can we expect you?"

"Tomorrow."

The dry airport air felt like it was suffocating me.

I was just heading home in fear that Dean hurt himself by

suicide or overdose, but no. He killed someone else. He would have killed me. I was right.

Millions of questions consumed me, and I couldn't move. I didn't have the emotional capacity to handle what I felt.

Ella was holding my arm. "Nikki, what happened? Nikki..."

A living, breathing horror movie was blaring in my mind. *What happened? What could she have done? Did he strangle her, or did he shoot her? Was he even alive now?* Suddenly, I snapped out of the movie in my mind and came back to my senses. "Dean killed someone in my home. Now he's on the run."

Saying that out loud spun me into a panic attack. I could hear my heart beating, and I began to wobble. I desperately chewed Valium without water. Ella helped me sit down where I cried and collected myself. "You will get through this. You're going to be okay." She was right; I was, but I was on a constant stream of Valium to prevent breaking all the way down. I couldn't believe this was my reality. I couldn't believe I just left him weeks six ago. I was overwhelmed knowing Gia had to live with the knowledge that her father was a murderer. I felt her future pain, and it was heartbreaking. I thought about the mysterious premonition Ella had that served as a guide for me to get the hell outta there; she saw the home with police tape and warned me. I was so grateful I got out, but I also felt incredibly guilty that another woman ended up dead.

CHAPTER 23

Landing in Las Vegas with Ella, I was notified that Dean was found and now in police custody. We took a cab to my car, and when we got in, I realized the pistol was under the seat. I had been in such a rush when I escaped that I didn't check. I took it out from under the driver's seat' and wiped it down with baby wipes and dumped it in a garbage bin in a nearby parking lot. We headed for the hotel to rest and recuperate before my meeting with the detective the next morning. That night I barely slept. I worried that the police may arrest me for what was at the home. I was going to tell the truth: that I escaped fearing for my life. I was abused. I wanted to end the illegal and toxic behavior a while back, and he wasn't going for it.

The next morning, I headed to the detective's office where I was led to a small interrogation room with nothing but a four-person table and white walls. I answered questions; luckily, the guys who were at the home at the time of murder also said I no longer lived in the home. My things were still in the closet and scattered through the home, but I had left them in a rush. The detective prepared me with what I'd see in my home. He told me the home had been torn apart to search for drugs, money, and weapons. "The incident occurred in the master bedroom closet. The body was removed yesterday, but there's still blood in the surrounding area."

Scrunching my face, I nodded my head and finally asked, "Are you able to tell me how she died?" I was not sure that I was totally ready for the answer. "She was shot in the head." My stomach hurt; I realized he shot her with the TEC-9 since I dumped the pistol last night. The detective handed me a business card and pointed at the address. "Your other two cars can be picked up from the impound here." Then he handed me the keys. Ella and I didn't know what to expect. We made our way to my place. It was time to get it over with.

Pulling into my gated community, I thought back to the first time I had entered through the guarded entryway and fell in love with the lush landscaping and rock waterfalls surrounding the gates. I never imagined I would one day claim the keys of my dream home from homicide detectives, yet here I was. Driving through the golf course to my home, I considered that just days ago, the woman who died took her last car ride on this road. I wondered if she knew she was in trouble at that time. Parking in the driveway, I realized nothing felt the same. I took a deep breath and walked in with Ella by my side. She had visited the home once; we had fun, yet she also witnessed the dark side of Dean during her stay. She knew it all. This kind of darkness was different.

Stepping into the foyer, I saw that the home was torn apart. The kitchen was trashed. Every cabinet and drawer was emptied and strewn across the table and counter space. The idea of clearing the space defeated me mentally.

Exhausted within the first five minutes, I stood in the kitchen, feeling stuck. My feet and heart were so heavy. "Ella, *how* do I begin to do this? I don't know where to start."

The house was eerie. I felt a presence in the home. I glanced around, but no else was there. I shivered, even though the thermostat on the dining room wall indicated it was an arid eighty-six degrees. The place had been sealed up and was baking in the Vegas heat since the detectives concluded their investigation and locked it up. I cautiously made my way into the living room, stepping over papers and books that had been carelessly thrown onto the living room floor. Scanning the room for treasures that may have been treated as trash, I saw photographs peeking out from beneath the debris. My curiosity beckoned me to carefully step closer. As I obeyed, I realized the images were from Gia's first birthday party. I reached down for the tip of the nearest image and pulled it free. Instantly, I recognized the beautiful image; the brightly colored balloons lining the swimming pool gave it away. I remembered the day of the party; my daughter was turning one. I did a great job at pretending I had it together. I wore the mask well, for the most part. We hired the gigantic Barney and Elmo costumed actors for her. Back then, I still held hope for my family and our future. At any moment, someone can make a change and get better; I knew that, and I clung onto that idea like a floating device while I was adrift and lost at sea.

As I reached down to grab what was left of the memories scattered across the floor, my throat tightened and hot tears began to stream down my cheeks. I kneeled on the ground, fighting back the tears. I was crushed by the harshness of my new reality. I was truly alone now. I had felt misplaced my entire life, but this time it was different; it was worse. Taking a deep breath, I lifted my T-shirt up to wipe my face. I knew I couldn't get through this unless I pulled it together. I hated myself for crying; this was no time for weakness; I knew that walking in the door. I could hear Ella coming out of the bathroom. I stood up and reminded myself to toughen up.

The mess was somewhat expected but not the smell. Each inhale made it more and more real to me. The stench affirmed what the detective warned I'd find upstairs.

Suddenly, I decided all of it was trash. I couldn't sift through the mess; it reminded me of death. I didn't want any of it. Making my way around the massive kitchen island, I noticed a small mound of what appeared to be cocaine and two small lines cut out and off to the side. I dabbed my pinky in the powder and tasted it. Yep, cocaine. I decided to take it with me. I couldn't walk past it and leave it. I didn't care that it was dusty from sitting out for days.

There were definitely people partying and having a good time before the murder happened. *But who?* I wondered. We made our way upstairs. When we reached the second floor, I saw cocaine on the wet bar near the pool table. Yep, a party, but what the hell went wrong? There was so much cocaine confiscated in the cabinets that the grams dumped out on hard surfaces throughout the home were meaningless to the DEA. They didn't even care. It was like passing a penny on the street; they weren't bending over to pick it up.

I peeked into Gia's lavender room; my eyes noticed that they had emptied her drawers, yet I chose to look up. I fixated on her beautiful crystal chandelier. For a moment, I allowed the grief in. I felt the broken dreams that once gave me hope. My daughter lived this lavish lifestyle I always wished for. That chandelier reminded me of my dream. The dream was over; the bullet hole above her vintage, white crib reminded me of that.

My dread stemmed from the fact that the dead woman found in this very home was meant to be me. The images of arguments and violence that led me to flee flashed through my mind, and I tried to shake them away. Opening the doorway to my bedroom, I walked in and stood at the foot of the bed. I could see the bullet hole I saw in Gia's room. It hit the center of the wall next to my bed. I cringed, thinking about him shooting and barely missing Gia's bed. My eyes scanned the room that had been torn apart by the detectives, and I noticed condom wrappers on the bedside table.

There were a few apple-cinnamon scented candles scattered on the dresser; they had been left behind and burned down all the way to the end of the wick. These weren't my candles. I felt chills move through my body when I realized they were purchased to hide the smell of death from all the blood left behind with her body. Even though the body was removed last night, the scent was strong.

I attempted to prepare myself for what I was about to see in my closet. My master closet was larger than many of my previous bedrooms. Ella stood a few feet behind me; she was allowing me to process as I went along. She was crying, but I felt empty and in shock. I couldn't allow myself to feel this.

I stopped to look out of the sliding glass doors of my bedroom terrace. I marveled at the feeling of peace happening just feet away from our property where I was doing a walk-through of the crime scene. The contrast reminded me that we never truly know what was happening around us. I attempted to calm myself to avoid panic but I couldn't escape the emotional grip of what happened in the room just days ago.

It hurt to think about, so I tried my best not to. "Okay, let's see it. I'm ready. Are you?" I looked to Ella because I needed her support in this. My trembling hand twisted the doorknob, and I opened the closet door. I looked at the closet window first and then down upon the six foot by three foot cut in the carpet and the surrounding blood and bits of human tissue. My legs felt wobbly as my mind processed what happened. They had cut out the carpet directly where her body lay and took it with them, but the blood seeped into the padding and onto the cement. I saw her gold hoop earring just to the side of the cutout. I wondered how long she lay in here alone before she was discovered. I thought about the people she left behind. If only these walls could talk. My clothing and shoe boxes still lined the room; I knew right away that I wanted none of them.

I had to leave; I couldn't think about moving everything into storage. I couldn't organize anything. I felt like I was on a bad LSD trip. I just needed to get out. I saw enough for now. I knew enough:

her life ended in my home at the hands of a man that a part of me still loved, even though I hated to admit it.

My imagination inundated me with violent images of her last moments: she was exasperated, screaming, and pleading for her life on the floor of my closet before being shot in the head. Did she know what was going on? Who did she think of when she realized it was her last day?

That could have been me. The truth haunted me. I imagined what she looked like, wondering whom she left behind. In that moment, as I stared down at her blood, I decided her life would not be lost in vain. I knew I had to break this cycle of abusive men.

I shut the door, and I told Ella that we'd have to come back later to work on gathering my things. I wasn't strong enough. As we walked out of the home and into the red rental car in my driveway, I felt lost. Walking away from my home where a woman I had never met was violently murdered, I had an overwhelming sense of guilt for being alive. I didn't know what to feel or how to behave. I should be happy to be alive and grateful that I escaped, but I felt anything but.

CHAPTER 24

"**D**ean left me to clean up all of this mess. He doesn't care about me. He knows I can't do this!" I cried. Even though his false identity was no longer needed, I still called him Dean. I cried to Ella in the car, and at this point, she cried, too. We were back at the house to make arrangements to move the furniture into storage. If I could've legally set the home on fire and walked away, I would have.

"Come on, Nikki. You can do this. You'll be happy you have your things, and you deserve them."

She was right. I didn't have much money left. I could use my things and sell what I didn't need to help me get by. We walked back into the house. I had the same creepy feeling as the day prior, and I sensed something was off.

"The TV is missing. What the fuck?" I was startled.

Ellas's eyes were so big; she must've been just as scared as I was. "Oh my god, it is."

There was a hole where the TV mount was removed from the wall. Someone was there since we locked up, so we ran outside and called both the police and the community's security. We waited outside for whatever help arrived first while the feeling of violation took over. The pieces all started to click. I lived in a guarded community that required guard approval for entry, and yet another gate required that people enter a code just before approaching my home. There were no windows open in the house either, so these details told me this was an inside job. It was either the community security or it was someone who worked the murder case. I started to feel like an idiot for sharing my plans with them because they saw that I was just a vulnerable, messy woman who was unable to handle the task set before me. I was honest with them about my plans when they came to help me because I didn't think about being robbed.

Now I was pissed about the situation and angry at myself for not pulling myself together yesterday and doing what needed to be done with my stuff. I never imagined the home would be robbed; it was locked and secured in a gated community. The Rhodes Ranch security arrived first, and I asked them to escort us through the home to be sure no one was inside. I was fuming. I couldn't hide my attitude. I told them how I knew this was inside job. "How else would someone get through the guards at the gate? Huh?" I yelled at them. I might be an emotional wreck, but I was far from fucking stupid.

As we walked through the home, I saw the TV was also gone

from the wall of the game room, and I realized I probably lost all the TVs. I was right. They removed everything of value, down to the Dyson vacuum and Dean's eighteen-inch wheels stacked in the garage in plastic. After the police came and pretended to be of help, they left without the ability to do much. I was angry at the savage behavior of whoever did this. My anger turned into acceptance as I decided I deserved to feel violated for my role in all of this. We waited patiently for the movers to transfer my furniture to storage, and that was the end of my home on Crooked Putter Drive.

Before traveling back to Pennsylvania, I decided to visit Dean in jail. I wanted answers, and I wanted him to know how deeply he hurt me. I risked my freedom to help build our lifestyle, and all I earned in exchange was abuse. Now I was left to deal with a foreclosed home and a daughter who I had to raise on my own, knowing I'd have to tell her this truth.

While visiting the jail, I signed in and sat in a room that resembled a greyhound station with chairs lining the walls. About fifty minutes passed, and I heard my name over the loudspeaker. I went to the booth where I signed in, and they directed me to a door where I could get buzzed in. There were phone booths that contained small black-and-white television screens.

I sat down, and Dean appeared on the screen.

"What the fuck, Dean? How could you do this?"

"I didn't do anything."

"So this is where you are. I already went to the house. I met with the detectives. I know everything." I was enraged by his response.

"I didn't do it. You'll find out. I need my mom to get me an attorney. Let her know."

He had the nerve to ask me for help while I was there cleaning up his mess. Literally. I just wanted answers from him after all that had happened. I wanted to hear him say he was sorry, and I wanted to know why everything happened the way it did. But I guess that was too much to expect in the moment. I even felt silly for expecting it. I left that night knowing I might never see him ever again.

The answers I desired came over time. After digging for information from Dean's customers, I found out who was with Dean the night of the murder. I was able to get in contact with one of the guys, and he gave me the details. I knew the guy; his name was Mack, and we met a handful of times. He was a good guy whose addiction led him to the wrong place. Crystal meth is a potent substance, and it turns out that meth was at the root of what wrong. He went on to tell me that our place basically turned into a party house after I was gone. He described Dean as becoming a heavy user, which blew my mind! He painted a picture of drugs being used around the clock, and strippers came and went; I believed it after what I saw in the bedrooms. Apparently, Dean was seeing the woman who died for a few weeks, casually. One particular night, Dean was at the house with Mack and another customer, Dave. The three of them were high and hadn't slept. After Dean mentioned he was going to pick up his girl, Dave started tweaking, which meant he was extremely paranoid and created stories. This story was about the woman Dean was seeing; Dave worried she was working with the police. After he went on and on, Dean started to believe him. He was pissed. Dean and Dave left the house to pick her up at the club where she danced; that's where the violence began. The two of them were questioning her, and she was attempting to escape the SUV.

As he described what happened, it made sense, and I put two and two together. When I retrieved our SUV from the impound to sell it, there were sections cut out from the backseat interior. The blood or saliva that was needed for the investigation must have been there.

Mack went on. He explained that the two men arrived home with the woman, and she was denying any association with the police. At that point, Mack wanted to leave, and Dean pulled out his gun and told him to come upstairs and that no one was leaving. The four of them went upstairs, and everyone was forced into my bedroom. They argued in the madness of their high for some time. Then Dean shot the gun a few times to let them know he was serious. As he described this part, I remembered the bullet holes in my bedroom wall. He gave her one more chance to tell the truth. She swore she was being honest. Apparently, she did her best to fight back, and finally, he brought her into the closet and ended her life.

After she died, Dean went into panic mode and threatened the men to help him or he'd hurt them. He ordered them to help hide her body, but then decided it was easier to try to cover it up and leave. He piled my clothing on top of her and went to get the candles from 7-Eleven. For nearly twenty-four hours, Dean watched the men and debated on what to do next until finally Dean went into the restroom long enough for Mack to escape. He climbed out of the kitchen window and ran away to call the police. His story triggered a flashback of my home. I remembered seeing the black fingerprinting dust around the window closest to the kitchen pantry, and suddenly it all made sense. The more I knew about it all, the more disturbed I felt. I knew Mack was a trust fund kid who spent most of his money on drugs, hookers, and gambling, but I sensed that he wouldn't hurt someone. I believed him.

Some weeks later, Dean called me, and he said he felt different. I'm sure he was sobering up and beginning to understand what had happened. He said that *voices* told him to do it and that it wasn't him; he said that "demons" were with him. He told me he began reading the Bible and suggested that I open myself up to exploring the teachings of Jesus. The conversation made me feel uncomfortable. He was an atheist and he knew I was myself. After all that had happened in my life, I doubted God. If there was a God that was all-accepting and loved me unconditionally, why had I been surrounded by suffering my entire life? That day, I hung up the phone with an icky feeling. This man had lied about everything, and now he had the nerve to shove God down my throat after leaving me to pick up the pieces of his mistakes? No fucking thanks. That April morning was the last time I ever spoke with Dean.

Seven months later, on December 1, 2008, I filled my black Acura TL with as many of our belongings as I could stuff into it. My time in Pennsylvania was too painful for me to find sobriety. I was in a fragile state; my mother believed Dean was innocent, which felt like a betrayal to me. My family and friends' addictions seemed to activate mine. I judged myself for escaping my problems once again, but I decided to listen to my inner voice. The same inner voice that told me it was time to leave Las Vegas now signaled it was time to go back.

Only this time I didn't have a place to go. I was down to only $800 to my name. It was risky to drive across country with little money to move into an apartment, but I had a plan. My parents agreed to keep Gia for a few weeks to help me get on my feet. I tracked down my friend Warren, who was still running his operation out of Vegas, and he was going to sell me some product. I was going to make money just like I did when Dean told me to go out and hustle.

When I arrived in Vegas just days later, I met with Warren, bought $300 worth of cocaine from him, and by the end of the night, I made an extra $1,000. I was ready to move into a new place.

By early 2009, the housing market in Vegas completely tanked. Between the murder and the market crash, my $889,000 home foreclosed at a value of $420,000. People who came to Vegas for the housing boom were moving back to where they came from, and the city was faced with an abundance of unoccupied properties. This was horrible for homeowners, but perfect for someone like me who had let my house go, had horrible credit, and needed an inexpensive place to live.

Within forty-eight hours of my arrival, I had a new apartment that I only had to pay ninety-nine dollars to move into. That's right, less than a hundred dollars to move into a two-bedroom apartment in The Lakes area of Las Vegas. Here's how that happened: ninety-nine dollars security deposit with the first month free! It was an incredible feeling of synchronicity and support. This was the beginning of me trusting I would be supported in moving where I needed to move.

In the following weeks, I sold my collection of designer bags and jewelry on eBay. I decided I didn't want the energy of my relationship with Dean or that time of my life seeping into my new beginning. I felt justified in selling those items since the money served us better. This money was getting me by and allowed me to bring Gia back, but soon, I was back to square one: I had a few hundred dollars. Previously, I had never worried about food, clothing, or paying rent. I had forgotten what it was like to not be able to afford my needs and desires. This was a brand-new type of hell for me.

When I got down to my final $300, I called Warren and bought some product. This time I didn't go out. I, instead, called old customers of Dean's that I retrieved from his phone bill online. After making a few thousand dollars, I felt like I could breathe again. I told myself it wouldn't be forever, but the weeks went on, and I found myself back in the lifestyle I didn't want to be a part of. It was a twisted comfort zone that I didn't know how to leave. I had an eighth-grade education and hadn't been to work at a real job for nearly four years. No one knew what I was doing. I spent my days with Gia and my nights drinking wine. When someone needed something, I met them in the parking lot of a nearby shopping center. Ten minutes later, I was home, and I went on with my life. I still got high, but I didn't need as much as my life was settling down. Mostly, I craved cocaine when I went out to drink with friends. Although my childcare was limited, I still went out a few times a month. One of those nights out at the club, I met a man named Jared.

This man knew about what happened in my home, but he still stayed around. He knew I had a very young daughter, and he still stayed around.

He also had a college education and good credit. He was playful and had a solid group of friends who were also like him; they were good people. He was unlike anyone I ever dated and that was also why I was insecure; part of me wondered why he was with me. While he knew about *most* of what happened in my past, he didn't know all of it. I selectively kept secrets.

He lived in Los Angeles, which gave us space. He visited Vegas one to two times per month, and he knew I had intentions to move to LA. We spoke on the phone every night, and most nights, I was drinking and doing cocaine, but he never knew. I didn't want to do this. I wanted to stop; his presence helped me down, even when he was in LA, as I didn't want him to know.

He partied, too. He was down for blowing lines on the weekend, but during the week, he kept his life together. The primary difference between us was that he could party for two days and live a productive life Monday through Friday while I could not. Of course, I presented myself as someone who also kept her life together during the week. It helped that he couldn't see me throughout the week.

The two secrets I kept were how I made money and how deeply I suffered from PTSD.

I didn't talk about my pain and fears because I didn't want to scare him away. I pretended to be over what happened, as if life were moving forward and I wasn't looking back. The truth was all I wanted to do was to move on. Yet, I didn't know how. When I lay down at night, all I could hear were my conversations with Dean. With my eyes closed, I could see the closet. I imagined the woman pleading for her life. I saw Dean standing above me in my closet with his gun. I was terrified. Every single night.

The night terror was eased by medications and wine. However, there was a darker energy that frightened me the most; it was the energy that Dean blamed for his madness.

When he claimed that "demons" told him to do what he did, it disturbed me. I considered the stories I had heard in the past of others who also blamed darkness and entities. I thought about what it took for someone to do something so horrible. It had to be *something*, right?

My fear was that I was also susceptible to this. I feared I would hurt my daughter or myself. My mind fed me memories of reading of the women who drowned their children or set their homes on fire. *What if this happens to me? What if it comes for me?* We lived in the same home; we were so close. Why him and not me?

I was afraid to be alone with Gia and not be on the phone with someone. I was terrified of knives, for I may hurt one of us with them. It was the most bizarre yet horrid affliction. I was too afraid to share with others, for I may lose Gia, and she was all I had; I couldn't lose her. So I stayed in silence, suffering and avoiding sleep. I stayed in the living room with all the lights and television on, watching comedies and drinking wine with my medication to keep me away from those crazy thoughts.

Eventually, the fear took over, and I had a full-blown panic attack when it was time to give Gia a bath. I feared being alone with her and water. She spilled ice cream on her shirt, her chest was sticky, and I knew she needed the bath, but my paranoia was overpowering.

I called Ella, and she consoled me.

"I know this strange. I'm afraid I might hurt Gia. I don't want to hurt her, but I feel haunted by what Dean said. What if something tells me to hurt her, and I'm not able to stop it?"

"Oh, Nikki. You're not going to hurt her. You love her. You wouldn't."

She stayed on speaker while I bathed Gia, and I saw that I was afraid of my mind. I created stories in my mind that were gaining momentum. Ella seeing me as okay made me feel better. She was my mirror.

While my PTSD was around in other ways and fear was a familiar way of life, I was now feeling safe with Gia. While I moved on from this belief, I felt shame for being so "crazy."

Jared didn't know to ask about my pain and shame. Talking about feelings wasn't his favorite thing to do, but when it came to my job hunt, he wanted answers.

Jared called me as I was headed out to make a run.

"How's the job search going?"

I was annoyed by his question because I realized I hadn't heard back from the applications I submitted online.

"Eh, it's not over. No interviews yet."

He wasn't letting it go. "Maybe you should broaden your search. There are always jobs. Be less picky, and you'll get one."

My tone changed to alert him to mind his own business. "I'll figure it out. Don't you worry about it."

"Well, I am worried about it. How are you going to make money? You are a mother. You should be worried, too."

Oh no, he didn't just point out my mothering. "Excuse me? I can't believe you right now."

My rage was beginning to show.

"How do you make money? I want to know. It doesn't make sense to me. You're never clear when it comes to this."

As he went on, I could tell he was accusing me of dancing at night.

"Look, I don't do that. If I did, why are you judging me? I get money when I need it working with my old customers, okay?"

He paused. "What do you mean by old customers?

"Remember what I told you about my ex? How he made money?"

"Yeah...selling drugs. What's that have to do with you?"

"Yeah, well, I connected with some of them here and there, and it's really easy money. It's holding me over until I get a job."

"Are you serious, right now? You really need to get your shit together, Nikki! You're a mother. No way is my girlfriend going to sell drugs."

His words slapped me in the face. "Who the fuck do you think you are by judging me?"

My anger clapped back at him,

"I don't want to do this. I have applied for jobs. I don't have a degree. I barely have work history; I haven't worked in a few years. You don't know what it's like. I'm doing what I need to do to make my life work."

Jared didn't know what to say back so he cut the conversation short, "We'll talk later. Gotta go."

"Bye."

I sat there with the phone in my hand, his words hanging on me like weights. How could he speak to me like that? He didn't know what I was dealing with. He didn't really *know* me. I felt violated, and I couldn't shake it. His opinion became a voice in my head.

You're a mother.

No way is my girlfriend going to sell drugs.

These statements felt like stab wounds. I was so used to being a mother who sold drugs that it became my normal. These two roles had been my life. I accepted it before my daughter was born.

I was so hurt by what he said. No one had ever said that to me. My ex made me sell drugs, even when I wanted to stop. This was my own form of normalized suffering.

I replayed those words again and again. Everything he said to me imprinted on the walls of my mind, and I couldn't shake the messages. I felt the heaviness in my choices. I wasn't with my family. I wasn't with my friends, and I surely wasn't with Dean. In a moment of clarity, it hit me—*this is how someone outside of my abusive circle is responding to my life.* My reality began to unravel, and I saw the truth about my choices.

Any sane person would have wanted nothing to do with the life I had been living. I was breaking the law and hurting myself and others. I rationalized that these people would be buying cocaine whether it was from me or not, but I recognized that was a bullshit answer. I could do better than I had been doing, and I knew it deep down. Over the years, no one batted an eye over my lifestyle, not even my parents or grandparents. No one seemed surprised about how I had been living. That realization hit me, and it made me feel incredibly sad. *Does anyone else care about me?* Suddenly I felt like I couldn't lose Jared. He was the only person to point out what I was doing to myself. I had been desensitized to the illegal way of life.

I called him back and thanked him for what he said. I was sincerely grateful for the conversation, although it was so difficult to be on the receiving end of it.

That was the last time I sold cocaine or any drugs. I decided it was time to get a real job and make money legally. No more hiding.

This was the beginning of me uncovering my victim beliefs. I saw where I blamed the outside world for my inability to get a job. I understood that, while no one was responding to my online applications, I was barely giving all I got when it came to obtaining a solid job. I was staying stuck because I was spoiled by making tens of thousands of dollars. I decided to put in the work and begin to dig myself out of the hole I'd jumped into.

That single conversation transformed my life. It was a fork in the road, and I took a hard right. Thankfully, I did. A few weeks later, I checked the mail and pulled out an envelope addressed from the FBI.

Startled by the fact that the FBI had my new address and knew where I was, my hands trembled as I opened and read the letter explaining that two of my phone calls were listened to during a federal investigation against my friend, Warren. He was now in prison.

My mind raced as I attempted to remember our last calls. I knew I wasn't buying on those dates; it was most likely asking him out for drinks. Now he was gone, and I would have been too if it weren't for Jared pulling me out of my own bullshit.

CHAPTER 25

If had to transition into the real world, and I absolutely had to, the only thing that felt right was working in an industry that didn't expect sobriety. I was doing my best to acclimate to the status quo. If I had to pretend to be normal, whatever that was, then I couldn't do it in an office. I wasn't ready to play that game, not yet.

This time I wouldn't be getting people high, I'd be getting them drunk. I was not sure that was better, but it was legal. I enrolled in a bartending class. One bartending class I found offered potential job placement upon completion, which lured me in. Despite the fact that I felt confident I would get a job regardless of whether I took the course, I still decided to invest in my own learning. The classes were held in a run-down, two-story strip mall in a shady part of town on Sahara Boulevard. It was gross, and the place smelled a bit funky, like an old basement.

Two weeks later, when the job placement wasn't panning out and my money was almost gone, I decided to take matters in my own hands and get a job. My long-term goal was to land a job at a nightclub, but at my skill level, I knew I would be crushed in a setting like that. I noticed how fast the servers were at the busy nightclubs. Plus, I had never been behind a real bar before, so I decided instead that a local gaming bar would be best to start.

Across the city, we had gaming bars. After having hung out at various locations for food and drinks, I knew these restaurants were open for twenty-four hours, so there were always people there. In a twenty-four-hour city like Las Vegas, there were people getting off work at all hours of the day who needed a drink. If you sat at the bar and put twenty dollars in the video poker machine, you could drink for free while you played. This amenity kept locals coming in and gambling. The main gaming bar was PT's; they had locations everywhere.

Determined to get hired that day, I decided to straighten my long black hair, put on my favorite skinny jeans and cute skimpy top along with four-inch black heels, and find myself a job. I knew what to do. I wore my best push-up bra and put my best attempt forth to create cleavage with my A-cup breasts. I generously applied my sparkly pink Chanel lip-gloss and gave myself a pep talk.

I felt sexy, and for that reason, I knew the men running the bar would hear me out. I drove to the location on Jones Boulevard, and I walked into a somewhat empty bar at two p.m. on a Monday afternoon. I stood at the edge of the bar until a cute blonde female bartender walked up and took my order. I asked for the manager and told her I was interested in a job. I was bummed when she told me that they didn't hire directly. I had to visit their corporate office, but I was relieved to hear that this office was close by.

The bar seemed big and bit intimidating, and I really didn't know what I was doing. I turned on Jay-Z and bumped the music loud enough so that it drowned out the mental noise, and I went into warrior, make-it-happen mode. Arriving at the corporate office, I walked into a reception area that felt like a doctor's office. A stack of application packets was on a table. I thought, *I'm going to be nothing but a damn number. A number with no experience. No.* I pushed away the doubts and remembered the pep talk I had with myself. I picked up the application packet and worked on completing it. Everything was going great until I opened it up to the section titled, "Work History." *Damn it.*

The mental block cleared as it hit me; I could list the strip club I worked at in Philly. Ownership had changed, and it was a basic Jack and Coke type of bar. That bar didn't even have martini glasses, which was embarrassing for me, yet perfect for the story I needed to create. This was survival in action. I was going to make it happen at all costs. I listed my former bar as an employer, which was sort of true. I listed a former manager who I knew wasn't there anymore and jotted down six months as an employee. Boom. I had this covered. The best part of listing that I worked there was that they wouldn't have expected me to be a highly-seasoned bartender from such a place. I felt a shift inside, and my confidence was back.

Just as I was about to finish my application, a tall handsome man walked into the room. I immediately recognized him from the photos on the entrance wall. He was one of the managing partners. He glanced over, stopped in his tracks, and asked what I was applying for.

I responded, "Bartender."

He replied, "Wonderful. Where did you work?"

I told him that this it was my first bar gig in Las Vegas. I worked in Philly a few years back. He was interested. He told me he wanted to bring me to meet the team and have a formal audition. Panic crept in. What did an audition entail?

One would never have guessed that they had, on the second floor of this beautiful corporate office, a mock-up version of PT's bar. Yes, they had a full bar with video poker machines, pool table, sound systems, and TV sets.

I was shocked by the whole experience, and I didn't know what to do. I felt awkward dressed the way I was in a fake gaming bar, pretending I knew how to operate the place. He walked me behind the bar and showed me where the bar stools were. He also handed me the various remotes and pointed to the bracket on the side with food menus. He explained that three of his partners would be walking in one by one, and I was to greet them as I would at the bar. I was to role-play greeting them, taking their order, and serving them.

Holy shit. I never expected this. I panicked and reminded myself of those risky walks through the airport. I pulled strength from the days when I had to do whatever it took to survive. This was no different. This needed to happen for me. I needed money. I was barely getting by. This was survival.

I yelled out to the men, "I'm ready."

The first man entered, and I said, "Hello, and welcome to PT's." It went well because the first guy ordered a vodka and Red Bull, which was one of my drinks. No brainer. Then it went downhill with the second guy. This man asked for a Manhattan up with a twist. *Nooooo!*

Up? What did that mean again? Martini glass, right? Fuck. Where was the shaker again? Twist. Is that lemon or lime? Do I still add the cherry?

I found the ingredients I knew: sweet vermouth and Maker's Mark. I poured both into a shaker tin and added ice. I shook vigorously, and when I was done, I poured it into a martini glass. To my absolute humiliation, the contents didn't even fill the glass halfway!

I looked at their faces and all three men were nearly laughing. "Short pour, hun. Don't you think? Oh, and you didn't add a twist."

Guy number two stood up and declared, "You never turned the TVs on, and you forgot the napkins for the drinks. I think I've seen all I need to see here."

Jim, the guy who brought me up, asked me for a few minutes of my time before he stepped out of the pretend bar with the other men. I felt the shame weighing me down. How could I have been so stupid? What the hell did I learn at the school? That was ridiculous. I hated myself for even attempting to do that. I wanted to find an emergency exit and dip out unnoticed, but I knew there was only one way out.

The door opened, and I was somewhat relieved to see Jim walk through. I wasn't feeling good about the expression on his face. He blurted out, "You know you failed miserably, right?"

"Yes, I feel horrible. I worked in a dive bar and…" I had excuses ready for him when he surprised me.

"We like your look. I like your personality, and I want to give you a shot. You've got a two-week training, and if you pass the same test in a live bar afterward, then you'll have the job. Deal?"

I was shocked. I replied, "Absolutely. I won't let you down. Thank you." Holding back my excitement, I went out to my car and celebrated alone.

One month later, I was working at PT's gaming bar, and I finally found my flow behind the bar. I did a lot better than I did in the terrible audition. I was sent to different bars all over Las Vegas to cover all sorts of shifts. When I applied for the job, I assumed I'd be sent to work at one of the bars near my house, which was a nice location with great clientele. Yet, that was not where I was sent because that was where they sent the best bar staff; there they had people who knew how to keep the crowd gambling. Their job involved more skill than simply pouring drinks.

I was unhappy because working near the Las Vegas air force strip during the eight a.m-four p.m. shift was not my thing. I didn't dislike it because the air force was nearby; I disliked it because the surrounding neighborhood was rundown. I ran the bar from eight a.m. to eleven a.m., and during that time, only a handful of customers would come in. Soon I learned that these bars were a hotspot for armed robberies. It made sense since these bars were also mini casinos. On the bar top, twelve to twenty video poker machines were being fed money all day.

Behind the bar, we had up to $10,000 for payouts on the winning machines. Between the hours of eight a.m, and eleven a.m., anyone who wanted to enter needed to buzz the doorbell and show their face on camera. I did have moments when I didn't let men in either due to a feeling I had or their unwillingness to look up at camera. I was still dealing with PTSD after all that had occurred to me, so this wasn't ideal for me. I snuck a shot of Ketel One when the fear became overwhelming.

Relief hit me when a group of men came to lunch from work and stayed for a while talking about sports or family. This was when I could let my guard down. I assumed no one would rob me when there were that many other men in the bar. After a month of being sent to only the worst locations, for the worst shifts, during which I only made sixty to one hundred dollars in tips, I decided to look elsewhere. I knew pool season was coming, so I opened myself to the possibility of applying at a luxury resort. *I deserve better.* This shitty job kept me broke. I barely made enough for rent, gas, and childcare. My other bills were piling up in my mailbox until I had more money.

Two weeks later, I had another wake-up call. Gia and I walked to my car at seven a.m. to head to preschool before my shift; only, my car wasn't where I parked it. *Hmmm, that's strange,* I thought. Our complex was made up of ten or so buildings with parking areas surrounding each. Typically, I could park in front of my place, but sometimes I parked around back. When the car wasn't out front, we walked around the building, and that was when panic set in.

Nothing! Our car was nowhere in sight. Then it hit me. The car was gone, and though I knew the payment was late, I questioned whether it was late enough for them to repossess it. My mind raced, and I felt the stab of regret that came from living in a deep state of avoidance. Now I recognized that I had to pay the price for it.

I felt horrible as little Gia asked again and again, "Where did the car go?"

Her innocence stung like salt in a fresh wound because it reminded me that I was behaving like my parents. Our cars were repossessed twice. Other times, my dad would dump them in the city and allow the streets to handle his burden as insurance covered the debt on a totaled car. An open car with keys in certain parts of North Philly wouldn't last long; someone would eventually steal it. I remembered asking questions about my dad leaving a car behind when I was a kid until I knew to shut up and go along with it.

I went inside to call my boss. My pride kept me from announcing that the car was repossessed. There was no way I could make it in, so I told him I had car trouble. Minutes later, I fell onto the bed and cried into my pillow, so Gia couldn't hear me.

I thought, *How will I ever make it back from this? Will life always be this difficult?*

A few hours and a glass of wine later, I gathered my energy and called my dad. He was irritated, but this was nothing new, it was less than a year since the murder occurred, and I had been skating on thin ice since. He told me to find a car ASAP. *No shit,* I thought. But how would I purchase it?

I only had $200 to my name so I wasn't sure how to pull it

off. My regular car payment was $320, and I was behind $1,300. There were additional fees to get the car back so my dad advised just letting it go. I took his advice and looked online for used car dealerships. Not only was money the issue, but also my credit was terrible. My home had finally foreclosed a few months ago.

My parents didn't have money. Neither did my friends. I only had one person to call: Jared. He had the money, but I wondered if he would help.

We were dating for a while, but I was still ashamed to share this news with him.

I drank some more wine and prepared myself to ask. *What if he says no? What is the backup plan?* I didn't have one. For once in my life, there was no plan B available. I needed a ride, and I needed a job. *Something will work out,* I thought. *It just has to.* I had to focus on the positive possibilities or else I'd drown in my fears.

I hated the feeling of needing someone. I despised it. My neck tensed as I held the phone to my ear. Somewhat reluctantly, he said yes. He loaned me $2,500 for a down payment. I waited for the money to hit my account, and then I'd catch a ride to get my new car.

I mentally prepared myself for this car. I called the Honda dealership where I had bought my last brand new car and paid it off in full within a few months. I thought Honda financing would see me as a loyal customer who pays on time. Nope. I also called Kia, which was known for its inexpensive cars and advertised, "no credit, bad credit, no problem," but I found out that also wasn't true.

I was left with the bottom of the barrel car lots who basically robbed you with interest, but, hey, what else could I do? I scanned the used cars sites and found a gray Mitsubishi Galant that wasn't bad looking. It was $6,500, which was reasonable to me. I looked at the location and realized it was at a small lot with only twelve cars and located on Industrial Boulevard, close to where Dean and I first lived together.

That stretch of road seemed to attract all things shady in Las Vegas. Strip clubs, bail bond companies, pawn shops, and used car lots were in the vicinity. People would only visit there when they were shit out of luck. Well, that was me.

A friend dropped Gia and me off at the sales office of the Chuck's Cheap Car lot. The office had one desk, three chairs, and stacks of boxes and paperwork that lined the wall behind the desk. Hastily, I signed a contract that allowed me to drive away with my own transportation. I was paying a harsh 26 percent interest on that car loan, which left me feeling violated. *Rebuild, Nikki. Rebuild. It's temporary.*

I had keys, and I could get around on my own. I consoled myself that it was all that mattered. As I pulled off the lot and onto Industrial Road, the AC was blowing warm musty odor that reminded me of a New York City subway. Tears started streaming down my face. I didn't know how much more rebuilding I could handle.

CHAPTER 26

Losing my car was a loud wake-up call to stop settling and make more money. The reality of the repossession also led me to sober up even more. I knew I was still sleeping through life. I was still too dependent on Xanax and alcohol. Cocaine was out of my budget, so my habit disappeared with my money. As pool season approached, I landed a gig at the Venetian and Palazzo Resort on the strip. All summer long, I worked at the pools of both resorts. There were long hours in the triple-digit desert heat, but it was worth it; the money gave me space to breathe again.

While my summer job met my needs, and allowed me to meet new friends, something bizarre began to happen by the end of the summer. I developed severe anxiety and vertigo. The frightening feelings would send me into a horrible spiral of fearing for my life. Gia was in the preschool onsite at the resort, which made me feel trapped in sobriety since I had to drive us home. I had to deal with it.

Most days, I could navigate the sensation and get back home. One particular day, it caused a scene that I couldn't ignore. The pool was emptying out, and I was waiting for my manager to close me out for the day. I felt tightness around my chest and neck like I was being squeezed from the inside. Nervously, I adjusted my bikini top to create more space to breathe. As I awaited my manager's arrival, I stood in the shade in my bikini and patted my forehead with a pad of cold, wet napkins. My heart palpated, and I froze. Fear overcame me, and I realized that an attack was coming. I started to pace, and I felt the world around me spin. I couldn't breathe. I considered Gia downstairs in preschool, and the panic worsened at the thought of me dying while she was downstairs. I needed help. I hurried over to my friend, Erica. "I don't feel good. It feels like I'm hyperventilating. Something is wrong." I started crying.

"Oh my god, Nikki." She was startled. "Let's call for help."

The resort EMTs came to treat me by taking my vitals and placing an oxygen mask on my face. I immediately felt better in their presence. I felt supported, safe, and no longer alone. After a few diagnostics, my vitals were fine; nothing was wrong.

The EMT spoke reassuringly, "It looks like you're in good shape. I'd go to your primary care doc as soon as you can. It may be stress. It could be the heat. Could be a bit of both."

"How could that be? I thought I was dying. Are you sure nothing is wrong with my heart?"

"EKG was fine. Get your daughter, go home, and rest."

Although the stress of being a single mother all alone with a four-year-old weighed down on me, I didn't see how that would affect me like this. My entire family had stress. I had even worse stress before! Yet, I never experienced these intense periods of paralyzing fear. I was embarrassed so I didn't tell Jared. I didn't want to add this burden onto our relationship. I had already talked about the murder, and I had no choice but to tell him about my repossession. This was too much. I felt broken, and I wasn't sure how to fix it. *Maybe I need an indoor job, out of the heat*, I consoled myself.

When I got home each night. I opened a new bottle of red wine and drank it, glass by glass, until the bottle was empty. The next morning, I would awake to the familiar scenarios that weighed on me, *I'm all Gia has. What if something happens to me? If something happens, she will be raised like I was. She will feel like I felt my entire life.*

The responsibility of my worries as a solo parent was stacked on top of all the trauma I stuffed away. Her sweet demeanor was a piercing reminder of all that I was missing out on. During these beautiful years of growing before my eyes, I was there yet not present. The guilt was overwhelming some nights. I was doing my best to stay alive and not end up in the hospital and labeled as crazy. I hated that I wasn't the type of mother who loved to cook and do arts and crafts. The truth was that I was barely making my eight-hour shift at work without needing a drink to feel normal again.

To make it all worse, I still hadn't shared my past with my new friends I met at work. This felt isolating, as I felt so much, yet I kept it inside where I knew it was safe. I decided it was best to have a fresh start and not carry the drama into my new life. While I wasn't totally over what happened, I would remind myself that all of *that* was in the past; it was time to move on and get over it.

My plan was to make money and create a better life for Gia and me. I would surely get over it. When the summer ended, I went to a new gaming bar where the ladies made out really well. It was a cool place; I had to wear lingerie, but overall, I was covered, and I was making money. All was well until one early morning when I came in to relieve the overnight bartender at eight a.m. The bar was unusually quiet; no one else was eating or drinking.

It was only me and the one cook, but he was all the way in the back of the kitchen. With no customers, he would remain outside smoking cigarettes and listening to music on his phone.

Bored and alone behind the bar, I settled into what I usually did to pass time: I broke down the wells and cleaned the bar. This was my quiet time to process life. I thought about Dean a lot, too, since he was someone who would have hung out in places like that to make money. When women came in, I wondered if they knew him or if he would have cheated on me with someone like them.

The silence broke when a man and a woman walked in. They were wearing all dark clothing, and it was dark in the bar, so I couldn't see their faces. I could at least identify them well enough to tell that they were white, and they gave me a weird feeling. Within seconds, I dismissed it as my normal paranoia and yelled to the back of the room to offer them menus, but they declined and went to sit in the back of the restaurant.

No one else was in the restaurant, and there weren't any other servers until eleven a.m. Normally, in that case, we allowed people to order drinks and food at the bar and take it to their tables, so I still considered their behavior acceptable. I told myself that maybe they just needed a minute to decide what they wanted.

Ten minutes passed, and I started feeling so uncomfortable. My body was signaling imminent trouble. Anxiety caused my chest to feel tight. I asked them again if I could get them anything. "We're good," they said.

I poured some vodka into a short glass and shot it back. Everything in my body was telling me I wasn't safe, yet I wasn't sure how to read it since my anxiety felt similar.

That's it. I don't give a damn if I am paranoid. I don't feel safe, and I rather be safe than sorry.

I push the red emergency button under the register to call the police. Relief swept over me with a slight twinge of guilt. What if they were just killing time?

Within four minutes, I saw the squad car pull up and two male officers walked in. I told them that I thought the two customers were behaving suspiciously, and since I felt that they were up to something, I wanted them out.

The officers headed to the back and spoke with the two people. Within a few minutes, they handcuffed them and searched them. I wasn't surprised by what they found, yet I was horrified nonetheless. The officer showed me that they had brought plastic gloves, hand ties, and a knife. They definitely planned to rob me that morning.

That day, I left and never returned. That's also the morning I made my decision to move out of Vegas once and for all. This time, I refused to run home to Pennsylvania.

CHAPTER 27

Three weeks later, Jared and I filled a U-Haul truck with my belongings and attached my Mitsubishi to the trailer. I moved into a one-bedroom apartment in Glendale, just north of downtown Los Angeles. The city was intimidating, yet I knew I had to get out of Vegas for my own wellbeing.

Gia flew home to stay with my parents for a few weeks until I found a steady job and brought in income. This saved me childcare costs, and I could survive on ramen noodles and bananas without guilt. I was determined to find my way to get my life on track.

After all that happened in Vegas, my move to Los Angeles felt like my happily-ever-after. I imagined that I had weathered the storm, and it would be time for the rainbows and sunshine. My standards were higher for myself, and I just knew that the healthy vibes of LA would rub off on me. What I didn't realize was that I counted on my external world to enrich and uplift me. I also counted on external love and acknowledgment from a man. In this case, it was from Jared.

In moving to LA, my once long-distance relationship became local. I imagined cozy movie nights, support, and intimacy that made me feel safe, like I finally had my person.

Life has a funny way of feeding us the medicine we need to become stronger and allow us to grow. We get what we need to evolve and to become a better version of ourselves, not what we ask for. At the time, I believed that Jared was the best and only thing for me. I feared I would suffer endlessly without him, regretting the one who got away. Comparing Jared to the men I dated in the past, I was afraid I would find myself with more men who hit me. What I didn't realize at the time was that emotional abuse can be as painful as being punched in the face.

My high hopes for our new local relationship dimmed as we approached New Year's Eve. He made plans with a group of his friends to get hotel rooms at the Westin Bonaventure and tickets to an event happening on the grounds. He didn't invite me; he explained it was a guy's night.

"Nikki, you should really do something with your friends," he said as if I were annoying him.

"My friends? It's New Year's Eve, and I've been in this city for two weeks. What friends?" This crushed me. Why wouldn't he want to spend New Year's Eve together?

"Like I said, it's a guy's night."

"Then why are the other girlfriends joining?"

He was quiet. Fuming and feeling the impending heartbreak, I said, "You know what? Fuck it. You have your night. I'm good. If you don't want to spend New Year's Eve with me, then why are we together?"

We got off the phone, and we didn't speak for two days. This was unusual because I would typically argue with Jared and allow my insecurities and anxiety take over. I had to reach out; I just had to. But not this time; I was crushed. I stormed out of the house to get a bottle of Pinot Grigio. I also decided to take half of a Xanax to ease the pain, and eventually I fell asleep, forgetting the feelings of betrayal. I vowed to leave him alone and wait for someone who treated me better.

Two days later, Jared called me and invited to the event. I said yes. Maybe my fierceness woke him up a bit. *It's about damn time,* I thought. The plan was for Jared to hang downtown with his friends to enjoy some alone time, and I'd join them around nine p.m. When we got there, I felt both excitement and an underlying nervousness about having been invited. My body told me something was going wrong, but I chalked it up to insecurity over having been rejected the week prior. Upon arriving at the hotel, I hadn't heard a response from Jared, and I had texted him around lunchtime. As I walked into the hotel, I saw the group of guys standing at the lobby bar. Jared seemed to be avoiding eye contact with me, and suddenly I knew it: trouble was coming.

This behavior left me stunned, but I told myself to remain cool since it was New Year's Eve. *Let's give this a chance,* I told myself.

Maybe it's in my head. That was the thing I realized about my relationship with Jared: he always made me feel like I was the one who needed to change. I was always too much of something or other for him.

I ordered my drink and said my hellos and gave hugs. I could tell the guys had been doing blow and that they were wired—their eyes said it all. Although I wanted some, I knew that in the situation I was in with Jared, getting high would be destructive.

If I drank and got high, the adrenaline rush of the cocaine would have pushed me into reaction mode. While I was sober, I could see that he was just being an asshole. Jared and I had intense fights while we were in Las Vegas. I punched Jared in the face inside the Palms Casino when he ignored me for twenty minutes while he spoke to my girlfriend. I was asking him a question, and he just sat there across the table from me, avoiding my eyes and ignoring my words while he pretended I wasn't there. It was so painful when I was drunk; the rush of the cocaine had me hypersensitive and on edge. The pain sparked the rage I felt toward him for treating me that way, and I punched him right in the jaw. I was shocked that I did it, and in that moment, I realized that I was not only a victim but also an abuser. Maybe I always had been, but the men in my life had always beat me to it. The roles changed in that moment, and I was horrified to see it happen. I knew it was wrong, yet if I am honest, I felt being punched was less painful than being purposely ignored, which, to me, felt excruciating. That was a major wake-up call for me.

I came to learn that Jared's abuse was emotional; I learned that abuse could mean more than the physical or verbal rage that I was accustomed to. I knew through my experiences with Jared that the most painful thing of all was the feeling that I was being totally shut out. It surprised me that we made it past that night, but the truth was that with him another unhealthy dynamic developed.

As our New Year's celebration continued, I barely spoke to Jared, and it wasn't by choice. He was in his own world, and I could tell he was being a brat. With each moment, I grew more frustrated.

Sipping my cocktail, I wondered whether things would have been different if I had worn a different dress or done my hair differently. Maybe if I were prettier, he wouldn't treat me this way. What could I say or be that would finally please him? I didn't know. I did my best to continue pretending that I barely noticed his asshole behavior, but in time, it became more awkward for everyone.

We moved outdoors to the secondary event space where the lights were bright and blue and white and balloons were everywhere. House music was playing, and the party was just beginning to kick off. The energy of New Year's Eve was in the air, complete with the hope of new resolutions and excitement for what was to come.

My face was red hot, and I stood by a tall white table, checking my phone and texting friends on the East Coast. Again, I was doing my very best to not explode. A pretty brunette with a cute smile walked over in a tight, sparkly black strapless dress. Jared enthusiastically greeted her with a hug and a joyful conversation ensued. The heat of my anger surged like an internal rocket of rage blasting off: three...two ...one. *How dare he ignore me yet become so thrilled over greeting this random woman that I have never met or even heard of?*

All rationale for staying calm left the courtyard, and I couldn't see straight anymore. Pain took over me. I felt stupid, and I hated to feel stupid. I grabbed my drink and stormed over to him, grabbing his arm.

"Jared, can I talk with you for a sec?"

He responded, "What's up?" He responded as if I were irritating him. This pushed me further.

"What the fuck is your problem? What did I do to you? Why are you treating me this way?"

"Treat you what way? I'm having a good time with my friends. I told you that you should've made plans with your friends."

If a human could've burst into flames, I would have in that moment. *This fucking guy. He finally invites me, but then wants to punish me. I get it.* I was livid and holding back tears at that point.

"You wanted me to make plans with what friends? You called me. You invited me."

His face was emotionless. He was so high that he didn't care about my feelings or me. He only saw me as a barrier to having fun.

"Look, I am here to have fun with my friends, so why don't you go do your own thing?"

He walked away hurriedly toward the building. Everyone looked at me like, *oh shit.* At that point, my eyes welled up with fresh tears, and I was bursting on the inside. It all felt like a horrid nightmare, and I wanted it to end. Some of the guys went after him, and the couple that I drove with came to comfort me. Their togetherness reminded me of what I had wished to experience at that moment, and the tears begin to flow down my cheeks.

After a few minutes, we walked into the hotel; we went up into the main concert room to find Jared and his crew. It was all too much. There was no changing where things were between us that night. I knew it to be true, yet my humiliation over the thought of going home alone to sleep off the pain of the night was excruciating. I wanted to try to fix it one more time.

Once more I approached Jared, thinking he might change his tune once he realized how I was feeling, but he got even more irritated.

He looked at me angrily and said, "Leave me the fuck alone."

I walked away, crying so hard my stomach hurt. The pain ran deep through my limbs and consumed me. I didn't know how to make it stop. I scurried into the bathroom to clean up my face and collect myself. Walking to the taxi line, the New Year's countdown began, and just like that, it was 2010.

CHAPTER 28

found myself in a new type of abusive relationship, but I failed to realize it because he didn't hit me. Because I loved him and feared losing his sporadic love, I adjusted myself when he pointed out the ways I was still not good enough: my job, the way I dressed, my weight as it fluctuated, and my inability "to be cool" when he was all over other women. His criticisms became my inner-voice. Jared's voice held weight; after all, he was the one who called me out and showed me how I was ruining my life in Vegas. He was a teacher of sorts; therefore, I believed nearly everything he said about me.

Each criticism became a to-do list, something to fix in order to be worthy of love. It didn't feel mean, because his words weren't delivered with violence. It felt like someone who saw where I needed to step up. Even though it wasn't necessarily mean, it still hurt like hell. I took it in because I truly wanted to be better. I knew that my being better would result in a better life for myself and Gia, whether he stayed or not, but I desperately wanted him to stay.

Building my life in LA was pricey; the quality of life was worth the cost, but this left me tight for money. Luckily, it wasn't long before I landed a job bartending at a new nightclub. In order to work, I needed dependable childcare, but I knew no one in LA. I knew there were amazing, capable women, but the work was in finding them. Could I trust them?

The club was on the rooftop of the West Hollywood. It felt glamorous for a bit; it was fun working at the new hot spot in LA. There was no drinking behind the bar, so it was good for me. In time, though, the newness of it all began to fade. The idea of celebrities coming into the club meant nothing to me; I also found that I was irritated by the men who grew progressively more intoxicated over the course of the night. It was flattering the first time they complimented me, but after the fifth time asking for my number, I felt violated.

I found myself sitting nervously in Starbucks with Gia, having coffee as she sipped her hot cocoa. That afternoon, we met with six different women who were potential sitters. I was interviewing young women I had found on Craigslist in response to my posted ad. Over fifty women replied to my post, but only six left a good impression on me. Now it was time to meet them and feel them out with Gia. It comforted me to know Gia was old enough to tell me how others treated her, although that didn't stop the shame and guilt of interviewing strangers from Craigslist to come into my home to watch her. Three of the women were nice, two were phenomenal, but the other was downright creepy. She brought a stuffed unicorn as a gift, but my body was so turned off by her presence, and Gia wanted nothing to do with the gift. I was so relieved when the woman left us sitting at the table yet concerned that she was now on the internet seeking jobs with other children. It took me a few days to shake the feeling away and all that my imagination projected for me, but in the end, I had two nurturing and dependable sitters.

Regardless of thoroughly checking references and listening to my gut, I would catch myself in the middle of my shift, counting change for a customer, being bombarded by projections of the worst-case scenarios at home. Vivid flashbacks of a *60 Minutes* episode based on a sitter who poisoned or suffocated children would take me over. In those sixty seconds, I would question everything. Why was I fighting so hard to make it in this pricey city on my own? Was it worth it? I knew it was, not because I said so, but rather by what I felt. I trusted my intuition. While I didn't know what my intuition was back then, I was being guided by my feelings. These choices felt good to me, and I was right; my sitters took turns, and Gia loved them both.

After each shift, once I had cleaned the bar and counted my tips, I drove home from the nightclub at four a.m. to pay my sitter one hundred dollars. After peeling off my faux leather leggings and black corset, I'd lay in bed, feeling conflicted. My body was completely exhausted, but my mind was racing. The loud EDM music from the club seemed to echo in my ears as I lay in bed next to Gia. No matter how exhausted I was, my PTSD kept me awake at night. I had flashbacks of Dean and me arguing in my home. I also imagined Dean standing in my hallway or strange men breaking into my apartment. Sleep was hard to come by, but I still managed to stay productive and get Gia to kindergarten on time each morning. My belief was that if I could stay up for forty-eight hours straight high on cocaine in the past, I could pull myself together on three hours of sleep to get my daughter to school on time. At this time in my life, I was proud of myself. I was making it out of my life that hurt me, my addictions were losing their grips on me, and I was winning, or so I thought.

Even though I was only running on several hours of sleep, I decided it was important to still get a workout in. My obsession to better myself began on a superficial level: my appearance. I didn't better myself for me; it was to be accepted. More specifically, I wanted to be accepted in my job as a bartender, which was based upon my looks, and by my part-time boyfriend who wouldn't commit.

I began to shrink in LA; I never saw myself as thin enough. I compared myself to the women I worked with and the women who frequented the club. Jared hung out at clubs like this constantly; I saw his lack of commitment as a declaration of me not being good enough. This worthiness centering around being thin wasn't new, but this environment magnified it more than ever. I placed my worthiness outside of myself, and by doing so, I abandoned my body's needs and my health.

I pushed through my harsh routine with espressos, energy drinks and Xanax. I noticed my anxiety was becoming more prevalent in the daytime. With the anxiety came other mysterious aches, pains, and neurological problems. My hikes at Runyon Canyon were interrupted with panic attacks. The open space, the vast sky that I never truly noticed, now scared me. I found myself avoiding hikes and soon the same feeling came with simple tasks, such as crossing the street. I found myself standing at a traffic light for twenty minutes in West Hollywood, afraid that if I crossed the street, I would black out. I was that afraid of walking into an open space. This was when I knew something was wrong.

After visiting my doctor and undergoing thousands of dollars worth of scans and tests, they found out was happening. I had agoraphobia, an anxiety disorder that led me to avoid places or situations that might cause panic and made me feel trapped and helpless. He described open spaces and public spaces as the primary causes of panic. My doctor was casual in sharing this information while I was having a hard time processing his diagnosis.

"Nichole, is there something upsetting you right now? Not here, but at home or at work?"

I looked at him blankly, wondering if I should tell him, but I decided not to open up, worried I may say too much.

"Not really. I'm not sleeping well. I work really late and wake up early."

"Hmm, well sleep is vital. I want you to know that stress is the leading cause of disorders like this one. See if you can start doing yoga or meditation. This should help."

Did he really just tell me to meditate? I want medicine for this.

"Isn't there something you can give me to make go away?"

"I can prescribe you something, but I still want you to work on reducing stress and sleeping more."

I blew off his suggestion of meditation. I couldn't see myself sitting still, and it seemed like a waste of my time. Instead, I decided to work on sleeping more. But after I left, I thought of his question about what was stressing me. I realized I was living a double life of sorts. I had years of my life that I hid from others. All that I stuffed away for years under heavy drinking and drugs was coming up for processing. Soon I was so sensitive and my inner-state was so fragile, that anything and everything would send me into an anxious spiral and often a full-blown panic attack.

I had so much trouble getting out of bed that I drank triple espressos for a boost, but still I struggled post-caffeine. Doctor after doctor told me "stress," and eventually I began to discount my symptoms. My parents had been stressed their entire lives, and yet they didn't feel *this*.

I judged myself as a hypochondriac when my tests were normal time after time, but I couldn't ignore what I felt. My hair began to fall out, and I developed alopecia, which gave me bald spots on my scalp. Some people told me it was trauma-based; others told me it was diet. Either way, I felt like I was twenty-eight going on eighty-eight. My health was deteriorating fast.

For once in my life, I made my health a priority over money and gave my two weeks at the club. But it was too late. That week I wound up in the ER because of a three-day migraine that wouldn't subside.

The hospital was cold, and the bright florescent lights seemed to pierce through my eyes and stab my brain. I was sure the hospital would uncover a terminal illness the other doctors must've missed. After taking my vitals, they had me sit in the waiting room filled with other sick people until a nurse took me to my own bed. I was in a bed directly between two other beds, with only a hanging blue curtain between us. It was a busy night in the ER, and there were cries and moans surrounding me. I hoped I wasn't here to receive the worst news of my life. I called on God, although I wasn't sure how I felt about him.

My arm was sore from the IV pumping cold fluids into my arm. Just as I began to doze off to the sounds of the machines beeping all around me, the hospital doctor opened the curtains and walked in to greet me. He was a friendly and frank older man. The hair he had left was all white.

"Ah, it looks like you have mononucleosis. First time?"

I had no idea what he was talking about, but it sounded treatable.

"No…"

"Mono. It's a virus, known as the kissing disease. You become extremely fatigued and sometimes it causes more severe symptoms. It's also highly contagious."

"But, wait, I didn't kiss anyone except for my daughter recently?"

"Oh, you probably pushed your adrenals with stress…"

He went on to explain that it didn't matter that I hadn't kissed anyone; it was a virus that could have lived dormant in my body like chickenpox. He said that stress, illness, and lack of sleep for an extended period could have triggered this. If Gia had it, she would have had different symptoms due to her immune system. My immune system was wrecked. He told me that it would be best to rest and drink plenty of fluids. He told me there was no cure or medicine so I had to heal on my own, which would take time. *Time? I need to make money to survive. What if I lose everything?* I felt the anxiety building in my chest and spreading into neck and jaw as I reminded myself that this was exactly why I am sick.

CHAPTER 29

My recovery time was intense. I had never been by myself without running. The mono required me to care for my body, so there was no drinking. Because of my desire to heal, I was weening myself off Xanax. During my three weeks in bed, I relentlessly searched the internet for ways to accelerate healing. To my surprise, I found meditation, yoga, and the idea of food as medicine.

Still, I was stubborn; I didn't want to go to these holistic places. If medicine didn't help, what would?! I had anxiety when I went to events. This resistance of what was best for me went on until I had no choice. I suffered a severe panic attack in the grocery store parking lot and woke up in an ambulance. My girlfriend Keri picked Gia up from school and then came to get me and take us home. It was then that I felt the true heaviness of mental illness; I felt like a burden to those around me. I knew I needed to change.

When we got back to my place, Keri helped me get Gia comfortable so we could have alone time to talk. I wanted her to stay. I was afraid to be alone; I was scared of what was happening. I was losing control of myself. The pressure of everything I had been holding in was surfacing. I sensed my secrets were killing me. The support of her picking me up from the ER made me feel it was safe to speak. I took a deep breath and let it all out. I couldn't be strong anymore, and I couldn't pretend anymore, not with the people close to me.

"I am falling apart. Emotionally and physically. I feel like I am eighty years old. I just want a chance to live a normal life. I'm breaking. I don't know if I can do this anymore. I'm so scared."

Tears flowed, and I watched her face soften. She didn't look repelled by my truth. I felt a sense of freedom by letting someone in.

As we sat at my dining table together, I shared more about my life, what I experienced, and the memories that were tormenting me. She was surprised to hear what I went through; she didn't expect to hear such dramatic details. After I finished, she reassured me that this would get better, and she affirmed my strength and dedication.

I believed her. She was right. I was stronger than I gave myself credit for.

Then she said, "I wanted to tell you one more thing. When I moved here, I was dealing with a lot, and my friends introduced me to a spiritual center that really helped me."

Shifting in my seat, I nicely turned her down, "I'm not religious.

I don't even know if I believe in God. I worry going to church would make me more anxious."

"No, it's not even like that. It's a happy place; the energy feels so good. Trust me, it's different than church, and I have a feeling it might help you. It helped me to look at life differently."

Keri was persistent. She pulled up the YouTube video of the center, and it was unlike the churches I had gone to in the past; this was more of a Hollywood production. The founder was a black man with long dreads, and the crowd looked diverse, from what I could see. "I'll go. I'm willing to get better."

When Keri left, I felt lighter. I let someone in and let some of my heaviness out. I relaxed in my bed with Gia, reading her a book as she drifted off to sleep. When she was asleep, I reached under my bed to find a book that Ella sent to me as a gift. I got *The Power* by Rhonda Byrne. I thumbed through the book, taking in its images. I liked the way the text made me feel. Originally I dismissed it as silly. *The power of positive thought? Really? That's nice...Is that going to make my past disappear? Nope.* That's when I shoved the book under my bed. But suddenly, the gift spoke to me. I needed to develop more positive thinking, and I was more open to change than ever; I needed a miracle.

Stopping at a random page, I began to read. After I read one page, I let it sink in, and I repeated to myself.

"Like attracts like..."

That night, as I was falling asleep, I understood I was being called to explore a connection to a higher power and to explore what this life was really about. I knew I was alive for a reason, and I sensed there was something important I was meant to do. I knew deep down that I wasn't alive to continue to feel sick and to struggle. I had close calls with death and prison; there was something important and meaningful for me to do. I knew a man wasn't waiting in the sky for me or judging me along with the gays and women who had abortions like a superior Santa Claus.

I sensed spirituality had to be greater than judgmental deities. I knew I believed in a higher power, but I questioned what that truly meant for me.

I thought back to the clarifying moments on LSD when I realized that life was bigger than what us humans had named it or defined it to be on Earth. I knew humans on this planet weren't the highest or most ultimate form of life energy in the Universe. Those moments of altered consciousness led me to call bullshit on so many beliefs I had been taught, especially those beliefs related to religion. No matter what I felt about the religious beliefs that had already been impressed upon me, I couldn't deny the miracle that was life. Much of my fears revolved around feeling totally alone. I craved a deeper connection, and I thought that would be from a man, but perhaps it was a connection to something within and to the power that animated me.

Two weeks later, I made my way to Culver City to visit the Agape International Spiritual Center. Ella was in town looking for an apartment because she was planning to move out West, so she joined me. Arriving at the center, the parking lot was filled with vendors selling beautiful art, crystals, textiles, and vegan eats. The environment reminded me of a small festival; it felt inviting.

I relaxed a bit. My church baggage was real, and I questioned the underlying intentions of places of worship. After taking Gia into the kids' room for arts and crafts, we went to find seats. The audience was cheerful, and the band was legit. I was surprised by the energy of the place and the welcoming of all races, sexual orientations, and religions. It was a safe space of no judgment and all love. While I enjoyed the message, of my power residing within in me, I cringed at the references to God, and the choir sounded like the one at church, but I reminded myself to see beyond it. I knew I needed to give the place a chance, I trusted Keri's advice. After the music played, the founder, Michael Bernard Beckwith, asked those who were visiting Agape for the first time to stand up to receive a blessing. As we stood up, there were probably another fifty or so other new people in the big, open room. The rest of the people seated in the room lifted their hands with their palms facing us. Everyone who was sat around us looked at us with smiles or with soft expressions on their faces and directed their hands our way.

The reverend led a blessing that everyone repeated sentence by sentence. It was so intense. I felt exposed and wanted to hide, yet it also was something I never experienced before. It felt warm, like love.

Thousands of smiling people repeated in unison, "You are a one of a kind brilliant. One of a kind beautiful!" I didn't know how to receive what they were saying. "We appreciate you, and we thank God for you." It went on for what felt like forever, but it was only sixty seconds or so of affirmations. My eyes were welling up with tears because the intimacy was almost too much for me to handle. I wasn't sure how to receive what was being said to me.

When the blessing ended, the strangers around me stood up to hug me and shake my hand, welcoming me. Their openness to give love reminded me of how closed off I was to receive it.

That first visit opened me up to what was possible, but the real shift happened when I attended my first meditation retreat with Agape. I was nervous investing in myself this way. I had spent thousands on purses to show I was worthy in the past, but investing in my inner world was new to me. I was pleased with my decision until I arrived and found out that I was to be silent for the entire weekend. *Silent? For an entire weekend? I can't do that,* I thought as the woman checked me in and directed me to my room.

The weekend kicked off with our first meditation. About 100 of us sat reverentially in a room, while Michael Beckwith sat on the small stage adorned with white lights and beautiful fresh flowers. He addressed us with the agenda, "You may have seen the signs that say, 'in loving silence.' I ask that you respect the silence and enjoy it. By the end of this weekend, you will come to know one another without saying a word…"

They weren't upfront about this! My ego wanted to blame. That night, I had to take medication to soothe a panic attack. The quiet was too much to handle; I wasn't used to being with myself for so long, listening to my thoughts full of worry, judgment, and fears. Removed from my comfort zone, I reminded myself that I could drive home tomorrow if I didn't feel better. Luckily, that wasn't the case. The following day, I understood why life led me here.

Beckwith opened up to ask if we needed support or had questions. I was scared, but I wanted to ask. I felt this was my only chance, but I had to be willing to speak in front of everyone. My hands were sweating. I was terrified of being seen. I felt small, and my heart was beating rapidly.

My arm raised, and he looked at me, signaling me to share.

"Hi, my name is Nichole…" My voice cracked with nerves. "I have been diagnosed with all sorts of things. I've been told I have a chemical imbalance, a panic disorder, and PTSD, and I've had depression my entire life. I hate the labels and the medication; I take it off and on. I worry that I'll need it forever. Just last night, I had to take my medicine…

A tear streamed down my cheek; I was embarrassed. *Who has an anxiety attack at a meditation retreat? I am ashamed of myself*

Wiping my tears, I continued, "I want to feel better, but I haven't been able to fully feel it. I would like to know if you believe it's possible to heal naturally?"

I instantly felt ashamed, as if I shared too much. My throat was burning from the pressure of sharing so openly.

With steadiness in his voice, he replied, "Yes, you can heal naturally. There are some things you'll need to do."

As he spoke, my helplessness shifted into hope. "Your biochemistry is changing all day long. Everything you eat and drink creates chemical reactions. The music you listen to, the books you read, and the people you spend time with affect you. You've got to let go of what doesn't serve you."

I listened intently as he continued sharing his insights. I listened as if I were being led to a hidden treasure of millions of dollars. To me, this was even better. This was healing. This meant mental and emotional freedom for me. He signaled for one of the retreat participants to share his perspective. A physician seated in the back of the room echoed similar advice. He encouraged me to eat very clean foods and practice meditation in my daily life. For the first time in a long time, I felt that things would be all right.

I hung onto the advice shared with me. His simple yet profound instructions were repeating in my mind all that day and into the weeks to come. *Everything matters. Everything that comes into my body and into my energy field affects me. I can heal myself.*

Now I understood what I had to let go of when I went home.

As I continued visiting the spiritual center, I could hear the voices of my dad and Dean. My dad would laugh at me and tell me I fell for anything. Dean would see me as a sheep. Yet I felt the grips of my anxiety loosening with each visit.

As my curiosity led me to explore metaphysics and spiritual teachings, there was a battle happening within between Nikki, the woman I'd been, and Nichole, the woman emerging.

Leaning into who I wanted to become felt uncomfortable as I watched the responses from people I'd known for so long. Enthusiastically sharing my newfound truths and possibilities, I was dismissed by friends. I'd respond to their complaints about common life challenges with law of attraction and mindfulness practices, and friends would snap back, "Nikki, I don't need to hear this positive thinking bullshit right now." After being shut down by people I'd known for years, I questioned my own advice. *Who am I to talk about this? Who am I fooling? These people see me as Nikki the cocaine dealer.*

The rejection stung. In these times, I wondered who I wanted to be. *Maybe they're right.*

Just because I saw the light, it didn't mean everyone else around me did. It wasn't their time, but at the time, I didn't realize that; I only felt I was losing the people who were a constant in my life. They still saw the same old me. This hurt like hell. I began to doubt my experiences, questioning if what I felt was real.

Jared definitely wasn't buying my transformation. We barely saw each other; it was once every few weeks. Each time I looked forward to seeing him, but I left him feeling more insecure and defeated. He rolled his eyes when I suggested he explore beliefs and behaviors that led us to fight. "Nikki, you're the last person I'd ask advice from on this."

Out of everyone in my world, I wanted him to witness my transformation. I found so much frustration in my need for his approval. Why did I still wait for him to call? In the midst of my internal upgrade, I still yearned for his validation. I was more fed up than ever with Jared, but when it came to this man, I felt weak, I was a sucker for this illusion of love. I admired women who stood tall and walked away from any man who failed to honor them as a queen. I wanted to be like Beyoncé in the "Irreplaceable" video, but I was felt more like Ashanti in the "Foolish" video.

These confusing interactions with friends and family led me to toggle between my former ways and how I wanted to be.

My changes began to feel isolating. But one thing I couldn't deny was that my anxiety wasn't ruling my life anymore, and I was feeling stronger.

The panic attacks became less frequent, and I was back to crossing the street again on my own without worrying. The mindfulness I developed through my spiritual practice gave me the ability to monitor what I was feeling before I spiraled out of control into a panic attack.

I noticed the conversations and relationships that led me to feel anxious. I learned that what I knew to be anxiety, was a message from my body. In time, I listened to and obeyed the signals.

I was doing the work on myself and experiencing results, but the healing took time. My sensitivities still showed up in unexpected ways. Being sober allowed me to feel more than ever, and I didn't know how to handle it. PTSD was the ability to relive the pain of the past in the present, again and again. The sensitivity of PTSD was something that you simply won't understand unless you have experienced it. An outsider telling me I was being ridiculous or dramatic led me down the spiral of shame and self-hatred.

At the movies with a group of friends, I realized I was too sensitive to watch guns and sit through the loud, thunderous noises of the surround sound. As the four of us sat in the theater, I shifted in my seat, pinching my hand nervously to keep myself grounded in my body and out of my head. When I shared what I felt, one of the guys laughed. "Oh my god, it's not real, you know?" *Asshole.*

"Yes, I realize that, but it's not me. It's my body…or subconscious fears…I don't know, but it's uncomfortable." Walking to my car, I questioned why I was so weird. These moments led me to dig deeper into understanding myself.

Over time, the tug within myself became more prominent. I was sick of Nikki; she got me into trouble. She led me into depression and heartache. She couldn't be trusted—not that she would hurt others— but she always hurt me. It was as if my very nature was destructive and disconnected. Desperate for affection, she was intrigued by the wrong men, time after time. But Nichole was much different.

Nichole was intentional. She listened, she prayed, and she focused on the possibilities. She also despised Nikki and was ashamed of her in more ways than one. For the most part, the persona Nichole could stuff away the darkness of Nikki, but it was only so long before Nikki made her way out into the world. Nikki was self-sabotage.

A friend came into town, inviting me out for a dinner and drinks. I had an itch to totally let go and not feel a thing. The itch came on when I saw friends partying through social media. Particular songs would trigger it and certain people from my past. The itch typically came when everything was going well, and I couldn't handle how different my life felt. I needed a dose of my past to bring me back to myself. I'd notice the ups and downs. The shifts in my behavior seemed somewhat harmless until I took it too far.

An old friend from Vegas was in town for the weekend and invited me to join him for dinner. While it was one of my favorite restaurants in Beverly Hills, I bargained with myself before responding to him. I knew I'd have a tough time remaining conscious with him; he and I were used to staying up for days in penthouses across the Vegas strip. My friend was a high-limit gambler, and my friends and I would party with him until we couldn't drink another drink or snort another line. *But that was*

Vegas; this is LA. It will be different, I told myself. He invited me to bring friends; I knew it would be a good time. After going back and forth with myself, Nichole versus Nikki, I reached a compromise. I would have a cocktail, catch up with him, and come home after a delicious dinner.

Later that night, Nikki was running the show. My friend and I no longer had as much in common. When my new interests weren't met with excitement, I drank more to be relatable. The four of us had consumed three bottles of champagne before our main courses arrived. Somewhere in between bottle two and three, I had asked my friend if he had Adderall, and he did, so I popped one. I had rationalized that it wasn't as bad as snorting a line because it was legal.

My pill had kicked in, and I'd lost my taste for Chilean sea bass, but I found myself ordering a dirty martini.

As we finished the last bottle of champagne, we decided to head to the club. I suggested going to my old job's bar; everyone was down. We arrived just before midnight, settling into a table together and ordered a three-liter bottle of rosé.

At this point, I was already drunk. The Adderall had lifted me, and I was functioning, but I was tipsy. I should have called it a night by the second glass at dinner, but I kept pushing through. I reached a point of not knowing when to turn off. We managed to drink the large bottle, and I suggested an underground after-hours club. This was one of the only spots to drink after two a.m. in LA. My friend called his car to pick us up, but he was too late, I was making an ass of myself at the bar before the car could arrive. As we walked out, I stopped to ask my friend working the bar for a shot of Jameson. As I waited for my shot, my former manager came out and told me no.

"It's too late. We can't," he repeated.

"Really?" The hypocrisy pissed me off as I remembered the countless times I poured shots for people after two a.m. per his request.

"Really. Not tonight."

"You know what? Fuck you." Then I walked away feeling frustrated and rejected. The reality of the bridge I just burned hadn't quite sunk in yet.

We piled into the black SUV and headed out to the after-hours. By this point, I was an absolute mess. The argument with my former boss stung, and I wanted to forget it all. Arriving at the after-hours, I saw my friend who owned the place and ordered a bag of coke. Within fifteen minutes, we had another bottle and a bag of powder we had dumped on the table to break into lines, and I was in a place of no return. Deep down, I could feel Nichole trying to communicate. I felt moments of guilt, but then I stuffed it away. I wanted to be free, even if it wouldn't last for long.

It was the first time I sniffed cocaine in over a year, and I was feeling right at home. I found what I remembered to be the perfect balance of down and up, drunk and wired. That's why I usually kept going until I got sick, fell asleep, or ran out of ways to keep going.

But that was before I met Nichole, this other part of me. Something was different now. The group of us did lines, danced, and sipped all our champagne, and it wasn't until I was making out with a woman that I suddenly realized how far I'd gone. I was still drunk and still high, but intense clarity came through. *What the hell am I doing?* I jumped as if I realized I had forgotten something important, and I did. I forgot myself. I forgot to love me.

"I've got to go…" I gathered my purse and called a car.

Hugging my friends and proceeding to run out of the club, I felt as if my skin was crawling.

I didn't know what I was feeling; something was different. Riding through Hollywood at five a.m. had a way of making me feel even worse. The homeless men and women sleeping on the sidewalks who had most likely come to California with a dream. I sat wide-eyed, peering out of my window, as my taxi continued to my place. The sky was getting brighter by the minute, and I knew that I wasn't sleeping soon. That was a hellish feeling. As I walked into my apartment, I saw someone jogging out front, looking like the image of health and vitality, and I wished I felt that way. Their energy triggered me even more. Inside my apartment, I dropped my things on the wood floor, stripped down, put on an oversized T-shirt, and opened a bottle of wine that someone gifted me months ago. I was relieved that Gia spent the night at a friend's because I was far from well.

As the sun shone brighter, I sat up alone in silence, drinking directly from the bottle, and gagging with each sip of the warm red wine. I didn't want to drink, but I had to quiet my mind. I couldn't handle the intensity of my mind. I was up torturing myself with self-hatred that no one could hear but me. Replaying the incident with my old boss, I recognized that ugly, angry part of me. I felt ashamed, and I could barely handle the heaviness of the hate I felt for myself. I worried that I would never be able to heal this part of myself. Scanning the night and taking in my behavior, I felt helpless. I knew better. How did I let myself do this?

A tear rolled down my cheek. "I'm scared," I said out loud to myself. Then I repeated it again, and this time, the tears came streaming down. "I'm scared!" The tears turned to agonizing sobs as I realized I was ruining my life. *Will I always be this way? Will I ruin my life forever?* Images of the people in my life who'd forfeited their lives to addiction flashed through my mind. The pain ensued; I was breaking my own heart.

I pulled out my journal. I started scribbling the thoughts that came to mind as well as the fear, the anger, and the helplessness. I was so fed up with myself. I was through with that feeling. I knew I couldn't end my life, and yet I refused to live that way.

Suddenly, I felt compelled to identify my highest self. I began to list how she behaved. It was a stark comparison to the past twelve hours I had experienced. I had caught glimpses of this highest self in the past three months. She had potential; she was strong and willing.

The depth of my shame and guilt in that moment felt unlike any other time I had experienced it. I was tethered between two worlds and between two identities: Nikki and Nichole. I recognized that, although Nichole was winning overall, Nikki was still strong, and when she showed up, I let her in.

I sat on my floor, sobbing next to my bed. As grief swept through me, I prayed, desperately asking for strength and courage. I didn't know whom I was praying to. *Please take over. Please take control. Please help me.*

Then it hit me. I was praying to the deepest part of myself, that highest version of me.

It was as if the tears and surrender had dissolved the fog, and I could see again. I saw that this highest part of me was whole and waiting for me to show up for myself. I was never helpless; I just couldn't see that through the fog. That highest me was always within, waiting for me to fully recognize the truth. She was guiding me all along, waiting to make a move in the dark times. I never sat down to hear her out like I had that night.

I felt a wave of peace sweep through me, and suddenly I knew I was supported in this effort to heal. I forgave myself for what happened. It was done. No more beating myself up. Only committing to change. I now knew the power was within me; everything I needed was within me. I had a plan, and I could rebuild and work within that plan. As I looked forward to the new days ahead, Nichole was leading us into new territory.

CHAPTER 30

O ver the course of two years, I surprised myself. With my sincere commitment to my spiritual practice, I was able to lead a life unlike anything I'd experienced before. When I left Vegas, I intended to leave my past there as an isolated incident that time would surely dissolve. For a while, it seemed possible. In 2013, I believed it was already done. I had successfully killed off my former self. She was nowhere to be found, and I liked it this way.

After the incident at the club, I surrendered to my spiritual practices and began to listen to my intuition. When inspiration hit, I opened myself to the possibility and took action. I became aware of all the ways in which I was limiting myself. Soon I saw that fear kept me stuck in a salaried position, so I transitioned from assisting one of the top financial advisors in the world to joining his team as an agent. I had learned so much from him, and I knew I was capable of sales, so I jumped in. While it was scary to take the leap, I knew I was able to do so much more.

For months, I jumped through hoops with the insurance commissioner and financial regulatory agencies to get licensed. My foreclosure and my criminal record came back to haunt me. Finally, I was granted my licenses to sell life insurance and variable investments, and my business was off to a beautiful start. Within the first month, I made $11,000, which made it clear that leaving my $6,000 a month salary was a great idea. The male-dominated industry was highly money motivated and competitive, and for a while, it fueled me. I allowed the competition to keep it exciting. I loved getting awards, and I wanted to win the free trips. Looking back, I was always great at sales, but this time, it was legal. Before starting on my own in the industry, I decided this would be my career until retirement. I had finally found something that offered unlimited income potential, and I didn't need a degree.

At night, I would go to sleep reading books on universal laws, and I began to harness my ability to manifest what I needed: clients and resources alike. One night, I watched a video on YouTube about children who needed a life-changing cleft palate surgery. The video explained that just $250 could change a child's life forever by providing surgery. That night, I decided to create a fundraising event and help many children. The energy from creating the event lit me up unlike anything before.

Since my business also thrived on networking, I met many amazing people. Soon my life was filled with entrepreneurs who focused on growth and giving back. While many people in my life asked questions like, "How will you get the money to throw the event?" or "Do you really think you can get 200 people to come? Do you even know that many people?" At the time, I was so grounded in faith that I knew the *how* was none of my business. I learned that I wasn't to worry about how plans would unfold; the Universe would handle that. My job was to remain focused on my vision, and that's exactly what I did. The resources needed for success came my way, I did my part, took action, asked for support, and soon it all arrived. I partnered with a pediatric plastic surgeon in Beverly Hills and the Small Wonders Foundation. We had a gorgeous event with a Grammy-nominated jazz band and a celebrity chef; that year we raised just over $30,000. This project demonstrated the power of a simple *yes*.

I began to wonder what else was on the other side of a yes, What surprises did life have in store for me? I marveled at the possibilities of what may be waiting for me to agree to and move forward with. After the event, with all its planning and excitement, something shifted; my financial services business felt empty. My numbers declined at work. I saw that I was no longer purely money motivated. I felt my life unraveling as the desire to compete with the other agents in my office no longer inspired me to perform. I didn't have a backup plan; this was supposed to be my forever. Somehow my forever was falling apart, and I felt afraid. Was I self-sabotaging?

The familiar inner voice reminded me of how I ruined everything, and I believed it. It became hard to get out of bed in the morning. The motivational meetings at my office that used to pump me up to make sales calls were getting under my skin. Seemingly overnight, I was fed up with the expectation of business wear: heels and outward perfection. I felt like a fraud in my office. I thought about the people who were doing business with me and wondered if they'd still do business with me if they *really* knew who I was. I decided they wouldn't. This curiosity extended to everyone who knew me in LA as Nichole; they didn't *know* me. I wasn't sure what was happening; all I knew was that my life was coming undone. This scared the hell out of me, but I didn't know how to reign in my feelings. Something was shifting deep down, and I didn't know how to turn it off. I wasn't sure if I should. I had learned to follow my intuition, and she was telling me this chapter was ending. I wanted to cling to what I created. I wasn't ready to let go of the best I'd ever been.

The unexpected happened when I woke up one morning with an intense desire to move back to Pennsylvania. Never did I imagine I'd move back home, not after how far I had come. For two weeks, I resisted. What was I to do there? I knew there were lessons that must be waiting for me there, but what? A man? Perhaps I was to support my family in healing? Maybe it was to mend my relationship with my mom. I couldn't be sure, but I decided to follow the feeling. It was one of the most illogical decisions I'd made, but by this point, I knew better than to let logic lead.

CHAPTER 31

Crossing the Pennsylvania state line from Delaware, I began to regret my decision. I received a call from my sister; we had a strained relationship for most of our adult life. This day was no exception. It hurt that we couldn't see eye to eye. I blamed her for our dysfunction; she blamed me. I cried when I hung up my phone realizing that there was no return flight to California this time.

My plan was to stay in my mom's place because she had an extra bedroom. I needed space to regroup and figure out what was happening with my business and get my life together.

That plan was short-lived as my mother's lifestyle and mine didn't coincide. Her late nights revolved around beer and loud music, which didn't support me getting my life in order.

My ego was bruised when I returned home. After working for

years to change my life, I was back to broke and worse than ever before. I didn't have my own place! I always had my own place. It was like breaking out of captivity, only to be captured years later and thrown back in. I had to start again. When I moved in with my friend, I was grateful. Her place was beautiful and spacious, but I hated myself for needing a place to stay. I started to think I was destined to be poor and struggling in pain forever. Doubting my choice to move, I wondered if I truly did overcome mental illness. I'd been listening to this inner voice, which now led me to my friend's guest bedroom in Pennsylvania. Maybe it wasn't intuition. Maybe I was crazy. One thing I recognized that I didn't expect, was the relief of being myself. I didn't have to hide my past or be mindful of what I shared. My friends and family in Pennsylvania knew about my past, but they still loved me. I realized how tired I was of living a lie. The role I played in Los Angeles was draining.

A few days before Christmas, I received an unexpected call. It was my friend, Bethany, from my days with Dean. She was struggling with addiction since our days of partying together. In fact, she stayed at my home in Vegas a few times. She and I spoke months ago, and I suggested she visit Agape and try meditation. She called to tell me that she went, and now she wanted to attend the New Years Eve Meditation Retreat.

"Nikki, I really want to go. No, I have to go. But I'm scared," she said to me over the phone.

It saddened me to hear her desperation, but I was grateful that she felt the strong urge to change. One thing I knew for sure: no one was going to stop doing anything until they were fully ready.

It did not matter who they were hurting or how badly they were ruining their life; it was irrelevant to an addict.

"Bethany, don't be scared. You're ready for help. Go!"

"Are you coming?" she begged me to join her.

"I would love to and I need it, but I just moved to Pennsylvania, and I'm rebuilding my life over here. A friend is letting me stay with her."

"No! I need you there. I don't want to go alone. Please, Nikki." I could hear the disappointment in her voice.

"B, you don't understand, I have roughly $400 to my name right now. Bills are behind, and I need to save for my own place. Things are crazy for me. There's no way…" I explained.

She wasn't taking "no" for an answer.

"I will have my boyfriend pay for your retreat, and I'll buy your flight with my miles. I just need you there. Can you come?"

Wow.

"Bethany, are you sure about this? I hate to have you buy this for me…"

And I really did. I despised needing help, but I also knew this could help me.

"No, seriously, I wouldn't go alone," she said.

Well, that was the benefit of living in Pennsylvania. I had help with Gia. I said yes. I couldn't believe that I would be able to fly to Los Angeles at peak flying season and attend the meditation retreat without paying. It was a miracle—unexpected—yet right on time for me. I was also grateful that an old friend was planning to change her life, and I was the person she called. In that moment, I saw that my choice to wake up was affecting my friends more than I realized.

Ten days later, I was meditating with 150 people at Joshua Tree Retreat Center. I felt the shift in energy as soon as we arrived on the retreat grounds. As I sat in silence, I reflected on my transformation. I was reminded it was absolutely real.

We sat through three days of silence until New Year's Eve. That night, a medicine family from Peru facilitated a beautiful healing ceremony. I surrendered to the healing with the intention for clarity as I welcomed the new year.

On that first morning of 2015, I understood that while Bethany had brought me there, she was part of a bigger plan. I had a reason to be there at the retreat. Michael Beckwith guided us through a final meditation together. My heart was full of gratitude for my miracle trip and the gift of leaving with a new perspective. It's nearly impossible to sit in meditation for four days and not view the world through a new life lens. I felt a deep peace that superseded the worries of home and the future.

In meditation, I allowed myself to sink in deeper. I asked for guidance on my next best steps. The silence was so sweet; I wanted to stay on the cushion for another few days. I caught myself wishing that the retreats were longer, and then I refocused back to my breath. Gratitude. I felt an expansive feeling sweep through my physical body; it felt like a high, and I also felt a presence. I saw myself standing on a stage with thousands of listeners before me in the audience. A subtle voice spoke to me in consciousness.

"Help women, and everything will be taken care of...."

My body tingled as I moved from my heart and back into my head.

What?

The information jolted me from the silence. I opened my eyes to come back to the safety of the reality. I looked around the silent room; everyone still had their eyes closed. *No one else heard that.* With my heart beating rapidly, I thought, *What was that?* I breathed deeply and went back into my meditation. My palms were sweaty while I reflected on what I heard. *Help women, and everything will be taken care of?* The feeling that came with the voice was all-encompassing and supportive. It reassured me; it felt massive yet safe. It was so beautiful and felt so nourishing that it was almost frightening.

My mind raced as if I had been told a secret that would change everything forever. I didn't know if I wanted it now that I had it. More than the words, it was the feeling. It was so much bigger than myself and anything I could fathom; the vision of the stage had a feeling. I did my best to sit in silence and go with the flow. *Who else has had this experience?*

As the retreat wrapped up, everyone danced to the tribal flute played by the Shaman and the room began to clear out. I gathered my things, still somewhat shaken by what I heard, and I approached Michael Beckwith to seek his council, and the tears overflowed. By this point, I had been to many classes and retreats, but nothing had happened like this.

"I don't know what just happened. It was beautiful but scary. I was told to do something, and I don't know if I can. I'd like you to pray for me," I said.

He had a smile. "Yes, you're scared because it's big. You'll have some serious work to do."

"I suppose so," I replied, but I didn't feel soothed by what he said.

"It's too late. You already saw it. You can't go back now. You can try, but you can't forget what you saw. You'll be okay." He smiled, almost amused by what was to come for me.

Walking on the trail back to my room, I stared out across the landscape with the crooked Joshua trees, feeling more lost than before. I wanted to focus on my financial goals; I didn't have time to help women. I decided, that day, that I wasn't ready to explore what this message meant for me, not yet. But here's the thing: life doesn't move when you say move. You move when life moves you. I was about to learn this lesson the hard way.

CHAPTER 32

The more I attempted to hold my life together, the faster it seemed to fall apart. As the world around me seemed to relate to me differently, friends I cherished seemed to fall away, and the small amount of business I was closing to survive in finance was dwindling to nothing. One afternoon, as I sat in traffic on the way to Philadelphia, it became clear that I didn't have to continue to resist. I could allow life to unfold without forcing myself in directions that weren't working. As I sat in bumper-to-bumper traffic, I referred back to my guidance. *Help women, and everything will be taken care of.*

It wasn't the first time I thought back to this, but it was the first time I was willing to let it take over my life. Since the retreat, I understood that I was to help women who were like Nikki. I was to support these women online. Women who felt trapped, lost, and burdened by their past. It became clear; my path of pain and suffering was the soul-shaping necessary for me to help others in this lifetime. The question that still remained was *how*? While that was my worry, I reminded myself the rest would be revealed as I continued to pray and declare that I was willing.

The beautiful thing about willingness is it creates a way. In my willingness, I landed a part-time job with a former boss that allowed me to work at home and covered all of my bills. Gia and I were able to move into our own place. But there was more. When I declared I was giving my life to this calling, I was Divinely supported in massive ways. This support also required me to trust my intuition as I was nudged to take action, even when I was scared. This meant that when I discovered an online business creation program, I signed up for the payment plan option and decide to go without furniture for another two weeks. Willingness requires flexibility beyond what you thought was best for you.

One of my favorite lessons in *A Course in Miracles* reminded me that I didn't perceive my own best interests, and it was true. At this stage in my life, I had surrendered to this. I would smile as the support came through to remind me I was on the right path. A friend learned of my devotion to helping women, and he gifted me a personal development retreat in Fiji that changed my life.

It wasn't long before it became clear how I was to serve; I was to coach women. Yes, there would be speaking and a book or two, but I was to support through coaching. That's when my doubt became loud. *Why on earth would anyone call me? Why would they choose me?* I had no certification. I had no fancy psychology degree. Hell, I didn't even graduate high school. At my core, I *knew* this was irrelevant. I knew my deepest truth whispered, "You were made for this."

The lessons I had learned in my lifetime couldn't have been taught in a classroom from a textbook. I had to *feel* all of this. I had to move through the full spectrum of humanness and come back to the light. It was in the late nights, with little sleep, when I practiced forgiveness around the people I loved who hurt me that I developed my coaching. Life was my teacher, and spirit was guiding me. I knew it was time. I was ready to take women through this work. There was no doubt that I was to help others; I was going to show up. However, as I crafted my bio for my site, I realized that I had left out so much of my truth that no one would know why I was built to serve.

Hey! I'm a former financial planner, and I've created successful philanthropic events. Trust me, I know how to create radical change in your life.

BULLSHIT, I told myself.

It left out my suffering, the pain that taught me my greatest lessons. I was missing my truth, my journey, the risks that it took for me to arrive there as the woman I was. Yet, I was afraid to share all of this out of nowhere. It felt like I was doing what Dean did to me when he came out about his past. I was coming out about my past; I had been lying for years.

I felt discouraged. I sat on my meditation cushion and asked: *How can I do this?*

Later that day, the answer came. It was so clear; it made so much sense. I could share through video, a legit video edited by my friend. I didn't have to tell people face-to-face or on the phone. I was afraid of the rejection and confused responses. The video would do it for me, and my secrets would be out once and for all.

The final step was sharing with Gia. I had to let her know before I shared with the world. *How does one tell a little girl who just turned ten that her father murdered someone?* I knew the shame I carried from this; I couldn't imagine what a ten-year-old would feel about all of this. Would she feel all that I felt? Would she feel worse? Would she wonder if she was like her father? Would she take on the shame I had carried? I had never been so intimidated by telling a child something.

Over the years, she only asked for him several times. Two years prior, we were at brunch with my boss and his girls when I overheard Gia tell them her father passed away. That morning, when we returned home I told her that her father was alive, but I didn't know where he went when we split up.

Now it was finally time to tell her. I decided it would be best to tell her while we were doing something she enjoyed. I made a special date with her and took her to the movies and then out to her favorite restaurant. I wondered if it would affect her appetite, so I let her enjoy her meal and then I brought it up.

"Gia, I have something to tell you. I want you to know that the only reason I haven't told you was because I didn't want to hurt you. I waited until you were mature enough to understand, okay?"

She looked at me with curiosity. "Okay."

"I actually do know where you father is, but I haven't spoken with him since you were two. He's in prison in Nevada."

She looked at me with a smirk, as if to say, *I thought so.* "I had a feeling because you said he didn't pass away. I thought he may have gotten into trouble." She was a wise one. "So what did he do?"

"Well, I wasn't there, but I can tell you what I know. He didn't tell me this himself; the police told me he killed a woman in our Las Vegas home. She was shot during a fight they had."

Her expression shifted to concerned. "I'm really glad you are alive, Mom."

"Me, too."

Gia had known that her dad and I had troubles, and I shared that he scared me, and that's why he and I separated. That day opened up beautiful conversations between us with lots of questions and some confusion, but there was also connection that can only be had when truth is involved.

On October 1st, 2015, I shared the video with my 2,400 friends on Facebook, announcing the launch of my new business. My announcement opened me up to support women while the video felt like coming out. My intention was to speak up for the women still suffering in silence due to domestic violence. October was Domestic Violence Awareness Month, so the timing felt ideal. I remembered what it was like to wish I had help. I reminded myself of the pain other women felt around the globe and found the courage to share. Others needed to know and to find the courage to leave and to accept themselves.

Sharing the video changed me forever. The act of showing myself liberated me. I saw that by escaping throughout my life, I wanted to leave the hurt parts of myself behind, but that wasn't possible. Suddenly I saw that the freedom I had chased for so long was here waiting for me to simply accept myself—all of me—the achievements along with pain and downright shame. I had to look at it all and acknowledge the gifts of my experience. I saw that I was not a compartmentalized being, that none of us are.

Openly sharing my truth of addiction, abuse, and committing crimes freed me from the past. It allowed me to see myself beyond those events. It felt like I had shed 300 pounds in that process. For years, I moved through my life in LA, hiding the hurt weighing on me, but I'm positive it showed. I was closed off in many ways. This video was my apology and my explanation of sorts. As I owned my truth, I could let down my energetic shield. I was able to look more people in the eye and speak from my heart.

The responses I received reinforced the need to keep going. I saw the power in transparency, not only for me, but for others who felt alone in their circumstances. I gave others permission that day; women knew they weren't alone. My choice to speak my truth was an invitation to others to find their freedom. The messages I received thanking me ranged from women who were healing from an abusive relationship, women working up the courage to leave one, to a man who had lost his sister at the hands her abusive boyfriend.

Finally, I understood exactly what the message meant ten

months prior at the retreat. *Help women, and everything will be taken care of.*

The months of my life seemingly falling apart and my willingness to unravel made me feel like I was losing my mind. I even questioned if I were bipolar at times, but I could see my life was falling apart to fall into place.

A greater plan was being pieced together. I wasn't able to see it until that moment. I realized that the feeling I labeled as depression was a surrender; it was the grieving of an old self, a former dream. There were parts of me that were falling away: the conditioning of corporate America not to show emotion and not to share your baggage, the illusion of perfection, and the need to pretend. All of it was so far out of alignment, and my body was speaking to me, asking me to slow down and listen.

Something shifted after I came out to Gia and the rest of the world. I had resisted my truth for nearly a decade, trying to remove my journey and to kill off my past. Suddenly, that which I saw as disqualifying became my strength. Within days of the video release, I recognized Pennsylvania was a part of my plan, but not forever. I'd been called home to heal; being home became a mirror for me to witness myself. During this time, I had a safe place to be myself without hiding, and in doing so, I learned to love myself more than ever. Within days of sharing my video, I sensed it was time to move on. I learned what I needed to learn here. Pennsylvania was the place I had to be in order to witness my transformation, a cocoon of sorts. I had learned so much about myself and the stories I carried with me throughout my lifetime. Realizing that these stories that limited me were never mine, I decided to do the work to let these deeply rooted beliefs go.

Finally, I'd come to see the lessons in the environment that shaped me, and I no longer despised it. I was able to observe it; this didn't mean I wanted to be immersed in it. Instead, I strengthened my boundaries and taught my family how to engage with me. I was now grateful for the gifts that it delivered. I would carry them with me proudly now, not because of what happened, but simply because all of it was a part of me. Each moment, each tear, and each stumble were meant for me. If it happened to me, it was perfect for me to go through, and I refused to deny parts of myself. They didn't ruin me; they unintentionally groomed me to do the work I do. I couldn't be a healer if I didn't learn to heal myself first. You appreciate the light so much more when you've lived in the depths of darkness, especially for as long as I was in the dark. The lessons now felt like blessings, but there was more work to do. I had a business to build back in California. I was still navigating my financial struggles, but I was ready to make things right.

My intuition signaled that I would thrive in Los Angeles, but I'd have to dig deep into my faith to make the move happen.

I sensed that Los Angeles was my soul home. I yearned for a soul-rich spiritual community, warmth, and the ocean. I was well aware that it was crazy to sell all of my things, uproot my daughter, and move to Pennsylvania only to move back exactly one year later. The money involved in our move across the country just one year after seemed outrageous. It seemed illogical, and it was, but logic isn't what miracles are made of. I decided I was making space for miracles. I reminded myself that logic is simply condensed past thoughts and experiences, and I was choosing to be visionary over logical.

As I worked on my confidence, I decided to visit my Reiki healer, Jeanie, in West Chester. After sharing my intention to move while disclosing my fears of making the wrong choice, Jeanie decided to pull cards and use the pendulum. We prayed and called forth angelic guidance, and she began asking questions. I was listening yet there was underlying skepticism on my end. Crystals and cards were fun, but I didn't give my power of choice away to them. Then she asked, "Is Nichole going to move back to Los Angeles?" The lamps in the room flickered three times. my eyes got wide, and from that moment on, I was a believer.

While the money to move wasn't in my bank account, I decided there was a way. I committed to moving in two months and trusted that if I did my part, life would support me in my decision. I was right. My business hadn't brought in a single dollar even though I was consistently sharing value and inspiring. The money was coming. I knew that. I reminded myself to be patient as I leaned into my divine message: *Everything will be taken care of.* Sometimes being taken care of requires you to take action and to take a step towards your blessing. Taking matters into my own hands, I went to a busy restaurant and applied for a bartending job. While I told myself I'd never work behind a bar again, I set my pride aside and made the money I needed for my move. As I prepared for my move across the country, I secured a job in LA to support Gia while I built my business. In the meantime, I submitted blogs to Huffington Post, and before the year ended, I got my first coaching client. I cried when she hired me, and I was elated by her results in our session together. The evidence that I was on the right path was everywhere, feeding my faith and building my spiritual stamina. The voice I heard back in Joshua Tree was my guide. I sensed magic ahead, but I had no clue about the intensity that 2016 had waiting for me, or else I may have backed out before life had a chance to make me even stronger.

CHAPTER 33

Gia and I set off for California in my Honda Accord. Our hopes were high for our adventures ahead, yet one small issue remained—I still hadn't secured an apartment in LA. I had called so many places on Craigslist with no returned calls. I applied online with rental companies, but my credit was an issue, so I was rejected time after time. I just knew I was meant to make this move; I trusted it would work out. I was willing to take the risk. I had a job lined up in LA. I had a start day, but I didn't have a place to live. I would possibly be homeless upon arrival with my ten-year-old.

The day before our scheduled departure, I was faced with a decision that required tremendous faith. *Would I move across country without a place to live lined up?* I had the money, and our furniture was already en route via storage pod, but this was a bit crazy, even for me. I'd done it before but never with Gia with me. I could crash on a couch, but I had Gia to consider. I called some friends in Los Angeles, and they reminded me that it would work out. By now, they knew me and these illogical decisions, but they also knew things tended to work out.

This is the last risk, I told myself. *I'm going.* My nerves were tense, but I leaned into my faith. My logical mind was going to war with me. Gia knew; she trusted; she was just as adventurous. I set the intention with myself and then got Gia onboard. We prayed and called in the perfect place to live upon arrival.

I made a rule to maintain a stress-free trip: "We will not worry about our apartment. If someone calls me to discuss an application I submitted, fine. Otherwise, we wait until Las Vegas to bring it up. Let's enjoy our trip." She was down.

If I had great credit, this would have been no problem. I knew the challenge with renting over the phone or online prior to my move was poor credit. Not only the foreclosure, but my fears around money prevented me from paying off my debt. I accumulated medical bills during the years; my anxiety led me to doctors all over Los Angeles. The scans and blood work amounted in thousands of dollars. I trusted it would work out when I met with landlords face-to-face.

On January 11th, 2016, we set off for our new life together. We hit Washington D.C., visiting all the spots Gia wanted to see, and then we ventured to Nashville for our first sleep. The next morning, we had brunch in the gorgeous atrium of the Opryland Hotel and made it all the way to Amarillo, Texas at three a.m. for our second sleep. The next day, we wanted to make it to the Grand Canyon by sunset, which was early in January, so we woke up at six a.m. and continued. Gia was so excited she didn't sleep at all until we got back in the car.

We made it to the snowy Grand Canyon, and it was as glorious as the year before on my trip back east, but it was colder. After exploring until our toes were numb, we had dinner in the lodge before making our way to our final sleepover spot, Las Vegas.

I went to sleep and knew that the next day required me to face the truth that I had conveniently pushed aside: we didn't have a place to live. I had held the vibration of being taken care of for the entire road trip, which meant I wasn't in fear or worried, but I was in full trust. I traveled as if I did have a place waiting for us. I was impressed with my ability to maintain this high focus. My spiritual stamina was strong. But the next morning, I woke up in Las Vegas, and the stress hit me like a shovel to the face. Getting out of bed, I walked to the hotel room window. I was miserable and began doubting myself. *What the fuck am I doing? How could I do this to us?*

We gathered our things and headed to breakfast where I began to make calls over coffee. Gia was in a great mood, yet I could tell she was concerned about me. I did my best to perk up and shift into optimism, but the pain of regret felt heavy. *We are homeless, and it's all your fault! Something's gotta give.* I reminded myself that I couldn't create effectively from fear. We hit the road; I figured I would get a place when I could meet the landlords face-to-face. Then, it hit me shortly after crossing the California state line: *I should call my friends in real estate and ask for help.*

So that's what I did. The first guy I called I had met through networking events; he told me he'd keep an eye out for me. The second guy I contacted was someone I knew a bit better. He was my friend, Dan; he turned out to be one of my earth angels. He explained that he had a rental unit available in the West Los Angeles neighborhood, precisely in Gia's school district, and he offered it to me for less than I ever imagined paying in the neighborhood. I couldn't believe it! It was such a blessing. After thanking him over and over again, he told me it would be ready in two days at which point we could connect and pick up the keys. I felt so supported and was so grateful I had the courage to listen to my intuition and do what appeared to be crazy. I felt silly for being so harsh on myself just an hour prior. This was what I call evidence; I trusted my intuition more than ever in that moment. I knew that Los Angeles was exactly where I was supposed to be.

CHAPTER 34

I had left California as one woman and returned as another. Returning, I was grounded in my gifts. I knew my mission was to awaken others to their highest Self, the highest version of who they truly are. I dedicated myself even more deeply to my connection to that which had given me life. God, Spirit, Source, whatever you may name it, it's still remains changeless. It was dependable and I was willing to trust more deeply. Upon my return I was diving into practices, books, and programs with teachers that would allow me to unlock myself further. I felt more liberated than ever, and soon I chopped off all my long hair. I was shedding more and more.

In LA, I devoted my life to my work. I invested all my money into unlocking myself and understanding that I was worthy of living my best life. I wasn't fully showing up like I wanted to; there was some resistance around asking for money from clients. It was easier to sell illegal drugs, insurance, and mutual funds than it was to sell my services to help women.

That year, I realized I could show up and inspire, but selling felt different. When I kept digging into why I found myself in perpetual financial struggle, I realized I had a lot of regret and shame around money. Deep down, I knew I was built to support others in transformation, yet in my deepest places, I felt unworthy of being paid for it. Sure, I could accept hundreds of dollars but thousands? The mere thought of it caused me to cringe. As I continued to battle with my own worthiness, I told myself I had no right to help anyone when I could barely pay my bills. Even though the healing process I took my clients through didn't require me to have money, I felt like a major fraud.

I didn't know what it was, so I named it a money block. After spending time studying online businesses that were thriving and understanding I had the tools to provide transformation for my clients, I struggled with the fact that I could barely afford to live. I stayed up into the early morning hours figuring out sales funnels and email automation and tweaking program offerings and my website copy. I endlessly asked the spirit to reveal to me how I could make more money. Fed up and ashamed of my financial truth, I felt like a failure and wondered if I deserved to serve others. I spent evenings asking the hard questions and crying the tears; I was diligent in moving through my limiting beliefs. I knew there was hope, but after all I'd been through, my inability to see my worthiness felt like a stubborn splinter I couldn't remove.

Night after night, I did the work. I faced myself in the mirror to learn more, fully aware that I was holding myself back. It was brutally painful at times. I often wondered if it was necessary to do all of this and to feel all of this. I knew I had to do the work on myself. The only way out is through, and I knew that. As my teacher would say, "This isn't feel good therapy. This is spiritual awakening." As my thirty-fourth birthday approached, I invested all the money I could gather into retreats that would expand my awareness. I could hear the voices of ex-boyfriends and my dad in my mind telling me I was so irresponsible with my money, but I had to do it. I needed to gamble on my gifts. I valued my potential more than other people's opinions on how I spent my money.

People close to me would say, "You don't need someone else to help you change. You're strong enough to do it." They were right. I was the one who brought myself through the fires of life. Yet, I knew that one insight was worth thousands of dollars to me. One shift in perception could change my paradigm, and I'd live a completely different life. I understood that I could get more money; it would be replenished, and I knew I needed to see differently to make the impact I wanted to make. At this point, I could feel I was a few decisions away from finding my flow. Just before my birthday, I decided to quit my job that I didn't enjoy because I felt called to go even deeper. I dove into next level soul exploration. I declared that I was ready to thrive.

Life supported me with an unexpected gift from a friend for my thirty-fourth birthday. Just like that, I was off to Costa Rica for a six-day retreat at Rythmia Life Advancement Center. I was going to explore powerful plant medicine, specifically Ayahuasca. I was scared; I wanted to cancel my trip last minute. When I arrived at Rhythmia, I wanted to back out of the Ayahuasca ceremony. I thought of telling them I prefer to do yoga and meditate on the beach, but I knew I'd regret coming all the way there only to back out. Luckily, I didn't. The powerful plant medicine allowed me to journey into the depths of pain that my mind had protected me from. The medicine was intense, opening me to visions of my father and his father. I felt the shame my family carried in real time. I dropped into my father's lineage and saw the innocence of him and his father and their struggles with connecting to people they love. This was the reason behind the emotional unavailability. I wept uncontrollably for the shame I carried around, the parts of me I had deemed as ugly, and the places I felt unworthy. My heart broke wide open as the nurturing woman facilitating the ceremony held me. Her hug was unlike any embrace I've ever felt. I was so raw and exposed, and yet she held me with unconditional love. The acceptance I felt as this woman simply loved me led me to cry harder. I was worthy of being loved. I was like an infant being consoled in my mother's arms. Hours later, after the colors and visions subsided, I laughed at all of it as I saw the love in everything I had experienced. I saw that everything was absolutely perfect, and I was free. It was an unforgettable experience. The level of surrender it took for me to sit in a circle of strangers in Costa Rica and drink the Ayahuasca was incredible. I shook as I sipped it. I knew there were messages I needed to receive; surrender gave me courage, and I was grateful for the wisdom gained.

When I came back home, I was hit with bad news. We had to move in thirty days. Our place was being renovated and sold, and I had just a few hundred dollars to my name. My family couldn't help. I held onto the idea that I could book a client, but as the weeks went on, it didn't happen. It made sense, as I was in total lack of energy. My spiritual stamina was wearing out; I was emotionally exhausted. With ten days left to move into a new place and now down to less than one hundred dollars in the bank, I had to shelve my ego and call an old friend whom I believed would help.

As soon as I heard his voice, I felt the shame of having to admit where my choices had led me, and I began to sob like a lost little girl who was attempting to find her way back home. That's how it truly felt. I knew home was close, but I couldn't quite find the way.

My friend wired me $6,000, and I was able to get into a place. In return, I promised my friend I would get a part-time job to help support me while I grew my business. My friend is one of the most successful people I know, a self-made hustler, so when he spoke, I listened. That day, he told me, "You can't expect to do only what you like; you gotta be willing to do whatever it takes for however long it takes. Later you can do what you want."

I hung onto that. In my mind, I thought it may take three years. If it did, I was willing to do whatever it took. I was in this for the long-term. In the summer of 2016, with my proverbial tail tucked between my legs, I moved to a one-bedroom neighborhood where helicopters and gunshots were fired regularly. I told myself it was temporary; I prepared myself for my greatest comeback yet.

In the next three months, I plugged away at my coaching business from my new part-time job. I was slowly making more and more money by showing up every day with live videos and valuable lessons for the people watching.

With the security of my part-time job, I went back to investing in my growth. I flew to Dallas for a life-changing seminar where I walked on hot coals, screamed at my fears, and decided I would no longer stand in my own way. In August of 2016, I sold out my first group-coaching program. It was the biggest revenue month yet; this gave me hope. I was ready for more.

Driving Gia to school in Venice Beach in bumper-to-bumper traffic, only to loop back around and drive to the Valley for my job, began to feel like hell. I kept this up for two full months, and then I started to feel on edge. I was playing small. I was capable of far more, and I knew it. Although I knew I made promises to my friend who wired me the money, I felt I could do better. I knew I could accelerate my growth, so I was willing to take one more risk.

I had been studying the law of vibration and quantum physics and gained a better grasp of my power to create. I trusted that I could create the same income that I was making at my part-time job if I gave my everything. Yet, I had the fear of failing, as I already exhausted my final lifeline when I borrowed from my friend.

It's funny how life works because I didn't have to make the decision; it was made for me. My boss didn't need me anymore, so he let me go. I was forced to step up in my business or get

another job. I went into fear for a few days, a\
I was living as a total victim of money. I had\
powerful than I was; I felt small and powerle\
making money, and I was fed up with it.

I journaled and prayed, asking for guidance.

I knew I was more powerful than my circumstances; I was willing to go all in like never before.

That week, as I committed to being more honest about my desires and raising my standards, the answers I had been praying for were revealed.

As I sat in Agape one Sunday morning, another awakening occurred, and the truth shook me. My hot tears began to flow as clarity washed my perception clean; I saw that I was one of one, and therefore, I was worthy of my desires. I saw that my value as a woman, mother, teacher, and as a healer was not my net worth. In a moment, I was able to witness my human value; I experienced my divinity. The tears wouldn't stop. I had to get up and leave the service to be with the information that came through. Wow. I'd heard the words before, and I'd spoken the words before, but in that moment, the information infused every cell in my body. I was made new in that moment. I shifted from deficit to divinity, and my relationships and business soon shifted dramatically. Life shares her secrets with us when we are ready, aligned, and able to fully receive their power.

The next day, I tripled my client rates for my next program, and just like that, I was full-time with my business again.

CHAPTER 35

nhaling the ocean air as I stared out at Bengal Bay, I couldn't believe I had made it all the way to India for the soul adventure of a lifetime. Taking it all in, there was a beautiful wave of appreciation for life and all that unfolded in the past year. I reached into my canvas bag and pulled out my journal and pen. Opening the journal, I wrote, "September 13th, 2017." I never imagined I would be in India after spending time in Peru leading a retreat with clients and friends. I was in awe of the path that I had walked over the past twelve months.

My coaching business went from $12,000 in revenue in 2016 to multiple six-figures in 2017. I served hundreds of women and men in live workshops, online group coaching sessions, private mentorship programs, and an international retreat. I transformed my finances, paid off debt, and moved my daughter and me to my dream neighborhood on the Marina. Gia and I were now living in the same area I once believed unobtainable as a single mother. But I did it! It was an internal switch with pure willingness to stop hiding from my power. I refused to be responsible for holding myself back from my desires. The past year taught me that my desires were previews of what was possible. More than previews, they were a direct call to action from the divine.

I began to thrive once I committed to never hold back. I embodied my truth; I am one of one. No one will ever have my exact makeup of experiences and gifts; therefore, how could I refrain from sharing my unique expression? Deep down, I knew people needed me. I was the only one who could deliver me. This is true for everyone, not just me.

As I spoke of this truth, I became a mirror for others to explore their potential. My relationship with Spirit deepened, and I felt I had constant communion. It was then that I realized there is an ascension from self-love to devotion. When I lived in self-love, my preferences ran the show; it was all about me. As I deepened my surrender, I began to lead from devotion. When I walked in devotion, I was living in full surrender to my highest potential. In this energy, I was willing to give myself over to Spirit. In this space of alignment, I was in flow. In flow, I opened up to grace and trusted that life had a plan for me that was greater than I could conceive. Leading from self-love, I was a driver, but leading in devotion, I was a vehicle.

In this expanded consciousness, I was highly aware of my

thoughts, noticing my fears and triggers. Instead, I asked the energy questions. *What am I needing? What am I afraid of?*

Sitting on the warm sand in India, I was grateful for where I was while never forgetting that there was always more available: more love, more joy, and more to give and experience moment by moment. In my reflections, I wrote about the boundaries I had developed that allowed me to become my own sanctuary, my own safe space to land. I honored the courage in the confused moments to trust life, have faith, and withstand uncertainty. Learning to embrace the full spectrum in life softened my heart with unwavering compassion. I laughed at the adventures I had been assigned to in this lifetime as I smiled and stared out at the grayish blue water, and I whispered, "Thank you."

THE END

MY LOVE LETTER TO YOU

Every second of our life we are able to create a new story, raise our personal standards, and say yes to the infinite possibilities. I am not promising that it will be easy, but I will promise you won't regret the times you choose higher.

Be willing to do the work to find your treasure, to be your safe space, and to be your very own, compassionate, best friend. Know that there are no solid rules to this game of life; we are all exploring. Even when we think we know it all, we surely don't.

There is a presence, a Universal Life Force, that has your heart beating and lungs breathing as you read this book. That intelligence is greater than our human minds can fully comprehend, but I can tell you that you don't have to figure out your life. In fact, you only have to let go and take a bold step in the direction you are called.

Give yourself permission to live a life that is undefined by your past. Trust that there is so much more to you (and life) than what you see. EVERYTHING IS REDEEMABLE.

Writing this memoir to reveal the details of my past was a brutal and cathartic process. There were several breakdowns where I asked myself: *Why? Why am I doing this? Why am I choosing to relive this pain and trigger myself?* Partly, it was for my own healing, but in the end, I discovered it was for you. It's for women like myself and the woman who lost her life in my home. It's for men and women who've forgotten their power and need a mirror to remember.

If I can forgive myself, then anyone can. Forgiveness is a spiritual synonym for FREEDOM. Forgiving yourself and others is the ticket to the freedom each of us desperately seeks.

Give yourself the gift, and do the work. Anticipate that Divine Intelligence will shake you up and release all that no longer sustains you. When the dust settles, you will discover who you truly are. Sometimes it will feel like absolute chaos, but on the other end, you will find magic if you are willing to be flexible when the winds of change blow your way. Stay rooted. With strong roots, you can turn within and drop into your inner-sanctuary. Here you will find a peace that you may not understand, but the good news is, you don't have to.

Use the following declaration when you're ready to let go and see differently.

RENEWAL DECLARATION // Reveal to me the ways in which I've unconsciously lowered my standards. Shine the light of my awareness on the spaces I've lived unintentionally for I seek to expand and love myself more than ever before. I stand in sheer devotion to what's possible for me. I honor myself, my mission, and my potential. I am ready to upgrade and uplevel in ways that are unimaginable in my current paradigm. I lovingly release all that no longer sustains my growth. I set myself free now, liberated into pure possibilities and the land of no settling. I am guided every step of the way; I am divinely supported. Moment by moment, I enter into higher harmony with my absolute truth. It is already done.

**XO
NICHOLE**

I love to hear from you!
Please send your responses and inquiries to:
Digital: nichole@libherate.com
Snail mail: Nichole Sylvester International, Inc.

Made in the USA
San Bernardino, CA
22 June 2018